THE
HAMPTONS
DICTIONARY
PLATINUM EDITION

THE ESSENTIAL
GUIDE TO
CLASS
WARFARE

MILES
JAFFE
ILLUSTRATIONS BY
PLINIO
PINTO

THE HAMPTONS DICTIONARY

Written by
MILES JAFFE

Published by
THE DISINFORMATION COMPANY
163 Third Avenue, Suite 108
New York, NY 10003
Tel: +1.212.691.1605
Fax: +1.212.691.1606
www.disinfo.com

— PLATINUM EDITION —

ISBN 978-1-934708-04-0
Library of Congress Control Number: 2008922087

Printed in the USA
10 9 8 7 6 5 4 3 2 1

Distributed in the USA and Canada by
CONSORTIUM BOOK SALES AND DISTRIBUTION
1045 Westgate Drive, Suite 90
St. Paul, MN 55114
Toll Free: +1.800.283.3572
Local: +1.651.221.9035
Fax: +1.651.221.0124
www.cbsd.com

for Norman,

who among other things,
taught me how to make chicken salad
out of chicken shit

FOREWORD

Accidents happen, and so did this book.

For years I'd been trying to capture the East End experience in a meaningful way. The essence of this experience is of course the irony that some of the wealthiest and most privileged people in the world are – at least judging by their behavior – some of the most miserably unhappy people on the planet.

Long ago I discovered that the kind of people who commissioned luxury vacation houses were all too often the kind of people who failed to pay their architects and builders. Years of this kind of experience took its toll, and in April of 2001 I struck back with *NukeTheHamptons.com*, enabling anyone with an internet connection to drop a nuclear weapon on the Hampton of their choice in virtual reality.

When the dozen friends I emailed the link to turned into a thousand hits the next day and with the global media attention that quickly followed, it was apparent that I had struck a nerve. Email poured in from around the world with targeting requests. Hundreds of thousands of people continue to visit the site each year, raining untold gigatons of virtual nuclear warheads right down on our very heads.

Ultimately, however, that mission was a failure. Sure, the Hamptons had been reduced to smoldering radioactive craters millions of times, but the intent had been to get people to think about their own behavior, and the closest I came to that was the choice of whether or not to push the button. Those most in need of a little introspection were the least likely to ever visit the site.

So I turned to another medium and tried to write about this bizarre unreality, in which Tom Wolfe's *masters of the universe* are simply *John Doughs* lost in anonymity among tens of thousands of the equally rich and clueless, the kind of people who confuse privilege with entitlement, the kind of people who make *Angri-La* out of Shangri-la.

One day, while reviewing some notes for an essay, I optimistically imagined that readers would be confused by some of the terminology I used. In my mind's eye I could see them scratching their heads over *hamperage* (the magnitude of a Hamptons event) or *philandrapist* (a real estate developer). The way to fix this, I thought, would be to make a glossary defining those words and expressions that might not be perfectly clear.

While jotting down a few terms and their definitions, a few more came to mind, and then a few more – soon I had well over a hundred. As I began to pay more attention to our language, specifically to how we use language here, I discovered numerous words and expressions that have been locally redefined, often in an ironic or sarcastic manner.

For example, while *The American Heritage Dictionary* defines *upscale* as *of, intended for, or relating to high-income consumers*, it is commonly used to mean *pretentious, overpriced or appealing to the uneducated palates of the nouveau riche*. What one person might call *upscale* and find attractive (such as a large neoclassical vacation house) might be something quite unattractive to another (a *McMansion*, *megacottage* or even a dreaded *Frankenhouse*). Thus the meanings that we individually apply to words is a reflection of our own system of values, which is itself the result of our daily experience, whether social or occupational.

Wait a minute — wasn't that exactly what I'd been trying to write about?

The Hamptons Dictionary had been born, and the original essay vanished faster than an empty parking space in East Hampton Village on a rainy Saturday in August. I had stumbled upon a way to write, in a specific and pointed manner, about the often neurotic behavior of the *ubër rich* and the incessantly aspiring *marginally rich* as well as those of us who must deal with *them* in order to earn our daily bread, make it through another interminable summer or even just the next four-day weekend.

The search for a Hamptons vocabulary was on. I pestered friends and strangers alike for terms they used to define the bizarre social conditions we struggle with here daily on the East End. I challenged everyone I met, even complete strangers, to come up with at least one term that I could use. A town cop described *Hamptonite* as a Mercedes Benz driving ignoramus who stops at the scene of an accident to ask for directions. The owner of a tennis club defined *tennis racket* as high court fees. A cabinetmaker explained *pillow talk* as empty promises made to a subcontractor.

The tables were soon turned as friends began challenging me to find specific terms for well-defined but as yet unnamed behaviors. I scoured dictionaries and etymologies, checking roots, prefixes and suffixes for clues to the word or expression that would describe in crystal clarity the behavior I was trying to name.

For instance, what do you call a person who is obsessed with the quality of their lawn at the expense of all other life on the planet? *Lawn* brings to mind *sod*, from Middle English *sode* (turf). *Sod* is also British slang for *sodomite*, which adds a degree of, how shall we say, immoderation. Add the suffix *–ist* (one who is or does) and you have *sodomist*, one who is perversely obsessed with their lawn. This describes a person who acts as if their lawn should be, at the very least, equal in quality to the greens at Augusta National on the opening day of the PGA tour (and God help you if you are the landscaper and it's not).

Overnight I became a word junkie, constantly on the prowl for a new fix. My office became a landfill of reference material ranging from Thorstein Veblen's 1899 *Theory of the Leisure Class* to McLaughlin and Kraus' *The Nanny Diaries*. I even read things I had shunned before, such as the style section of *The New York Times*, the weekly cultural guide for *sheeple*. Okay, truth be told, I didn't really read it – I just scanned it every week, along with some local *ad rags* like *Hamptons Magazine* and a number of other things I wouldn't normally be caught dead actually reading.

In this manner I discovered an extensive vocabulary – one that extends well beyond my own perverse inner dialogue – that brightly illuminates the shadowed underbelly of wealth and success. Some are existing words or expressions (like *upscale*) that have simply been redefined with a more acute and often ironically contradictory meaning.

Others are words that have undergone a slight alteration, often to just a single letter or syllable, that serves to create a new meaning, like *unvitation* (an invitation that is not meant to be accepted). Some are entirely new terms that have been created from conflations of two existing words, such as *cidiot* (city + idiot) or *waitron* (waiter + moron). There are also acronyms like *SCUM* (self-centered urban male), that have been created from the first letters of the words in an expression, and related variations such as *SPRICK* (spoiled rich kid).

Occasionally new words would form, as if by magic, out of old words or a new definition for an existing word would spring to mind in the middle of conversation. Most often, though, I would capture words and expressions from real life. *Do you know who I am?* is an all-too-clear indication of exactly what you are dealing with, whether you know their name or not. Some of these have been repeated so often they have become clichés. A few have become legendary, true *Hampton Classics*, the basis for stories that have been told time and again, often with stunned disbelief.

Many terms and expressions are double edged swords. While the *poor rich* are people who complain about the cost of everything that they can well afford, they are also those of us who somehow manage to hang onto a home (not a house!) here, and who by any normal measure would be considered exceedingly well-off. *The Hamptons shuffle* is not just a ritual dance performed exclusively by the working class, the steps of which consist of maintaining multiple jobs, or working double- or triple-time in a single job in an increasingly futile effort to be able to afford to live in the Hamptons, it is also the exhausting weekend commute between one's city residence and vacation house here. *Locals* range from people who have just placed a deposit on a Hamptons property to someone born on a kitchen table in Springs. *Local* is also used in a derogatory manner to indicate a person of simplicity if not downright stupidity.

Discerning readers may find a deeper meaning in *The Hamptons Dictionary*, a reflection on the effect of seemingly inexhaustible wealth on culture and society, for which *the Hamptons* are no doubt an excellent metaphor. But let's not forget that we locals (or those of us who like to think of ourselves as locals) are intimately bound to our guests. *Masters of the universe* and *counter monkeys* would not exist without each other.

While there is a certain element of schadenfreude in watching a self-styled *James Blond*, an *Uh-oh Seven* if you will, put on a *command performance* (an embarrassing public blunder such as getting one's Hummer stuck at the ocean's edge in an advancing tide), there is also relief; *there but for the grace of God go I.*

The Hamptons Dictionary was not supposed to be funny, and when you are suffering from *hummeroids* it most certainly is not. But with the clarity offered by a little distance, whether it be the sharing of a story with friends or simply the passage of time, it becomes clear that human foibles are the source of the most profound humor and insight.

Being judgmental need not make one either inferior or superior, it is simply an opportunity to reflect upon oneself. The question is not *"do you know who I am"*, but rather *"who am I"*.

Miles Jaffe

THE
HAMPTONS
DICTIONARY
PLATINUM EDITION

The higher a monkey climbs,
the more you see of its behind.

Saint Bonaventure, 1217–1274

ad rags

A-list *n.* A catalog of assholes.

accumulated wealth *n.* The definitive basis of self-esteem.

acquired incompetence *n.* The loss of ability to care for oneself or perform even the most rudimentary personal functions after adopting a lifestyle of dependence on BANANA PEELERS, maids, cooks, nannies, ESTATE MANAGERS, etc.

ad rag *n.* Any of dozens of landfill-clogging, advertising-driven free publications such as DAN'S PAPERS or HAMPTONS MAGAZINE that are delivered in superabundance to every real estate office, restaurant, antique shop and storefront. See **doorstop**.

addition *n.* An increase in the size of a house that is at least triple the area of the existing

1

structure. *What the original house looks like after expansive improvements have been completed.*

affluent *adj.* **1.** Less than wealthy. **2.** Having a net worth less than $10 million. *A disparaging term used by the wealthy to denigrate the merely rich.* See **wealthy**.

affluential *adj.* Having influence based solely upon wealth.

affluenza *n.* A virulent malady characterized by a voracious, insatiable appetite and complete loss of bowel control. *The reason MCMANSIONS have so many bathrooms.* Also **Wealth Disease**. See **consumption**.

affordable housing *n.* A house in the Hamptons that is listed for sale for less than $1 million. See **mobile home**.

aggression *n.* A primate behavior stimulated by over-consumption of resources and characterized by verbal or physical attacks on those perceived as competing for those resources, especially when those resources are in short supply. *e.g., Reservations at NICK AND TONI'S, bagels at Breadzilla, a parking space anywhere in the Hamptons during the SILLY SEASON, etc.*

aggrichvation *n.* The aggravation of having to deal with the rich. **aggrichvated** —*adj.*

alarm system *n.* **1.** A device for people who can't afford a caretaker. **2.** The illusion of security, especially when installed in a Hamptons VACATION HOUSE that is rarely occupied. Also **insecurity system**.

alcofauxlic (al·co·fo'·lik) *n.* A person who pretends to have a drinking problem for the sole purpose of sucking up to wealthy celebrities at Alcoholics Anonymous meetings. Also **psychophant**.

Alda *v.* To be ignored or rudely dismissed while seeking an autograph. *"Martha Stewart gave me an Alda."*

ambulance chaser *n.* A person who follows an ambulance for the purpose of beating traffic.

AMT *Acronym.* **actress-model type** *n.* **1.** One who makes a living based on their appearance. —*adj.* **2.** A woman with little intelligence and low morals. See **blank chick**.

anal bleaching *n.* The practice of bleaching the darker pigmentation of the skin around the anus for cosmetic purposes, often performed in conjunction with LABIALPLASTY.

Angri-la *n*. **1**. A weekend retreat for the never satisfied. **2**. A vacation house or summer rental that is too expensive to enjoy. **3**. The Hamptons during the summer, when tens of thousands of CIDIOTS and self-styled MASTERS OF THE UNIVERSE aggressively compete for parking spaces, restaurant reservations, coffee at Starbucks, a copy of the Sunday NEW YORK TIMES, etc.

annuity *n. Construction industry*. A poorly built house that requires constant maintenance. See **spec house**.

anonymity *n*. The condition of being a multi-millionaire in the Hamptons. *When everybody is somebody, nobody is anybody.* See **Do you know who I am?**

appliance garage *n*. A countertop storage area with roll up door designed to shelter indispensable small appliances such as a Miracle Pro Juice Extractor, Krampouz Electric Double Crêpe Maker, Impressa One-Touch Cappuccino System, etc.

architorture *n*. **1**. A Hamptons house tour. **2**. The futile practice of trying to satisfy the neurotic fantasies of the nouveau riche. **3.** A meeting, conducted loudly in a public place such as a restaurant, between a property owner and their architect or decorator, especially if using visual aids such as building plans and specifications. See **talkitecture**. **4.** Any McMANSION.

aristobrat *n.* The insufferable offspring of a MASTER OF THE UNIVERSE. See **bratitude**.

aristocrap *adj., n.* Expensive, showy stuff, particularly if mass-produced. *e.g., A McMANSION, BMW or Range Rover, etc.* See **noisy jewelry**.

aristocrat *n.* One who manages, without any visible effort, to thoroughly exasperate others.

arriviste (ahr·re·veest') *French. adj.* Newly arrived to wealth or social position. See **parvenu**.

artist *n.* Any competent service person such as a house painter, automobile mechanic, floor refinisher, etc. See **drain surgeon**.

assfluent *adj.* **1.** Capable of dealing with people on the A-LIST. **2.** Promiscuous.

assfluential *adj.* Having influence based solely upon one's sexuality or family lineage.

assignation *n*. **1**. An unoccupied house, listed for rent or sale, that is used by real estate salespeople for sexual liaisons. **assignate** —*v*. **2**. Designate a place for a meeting between lovers.

assoholic *adj*. A chronic asshole.

asspiration *n*. **1**. The desire to acquire objects perceived to belong to the social class to which one aspires, such as a LAND YACHT or a McMANSION in the Hamptons. **2**. The desire to get into someone's pants.

ATM *Acronym*. **Automatic Teller Machine** *n*. A rich boyfriend.

au pair *n*. **1**. An attractive young woman working as a surrogate mother. See **nanny**. **2**. Nice tits.

august *adj*. **1**. Extreme, over the top. *"The traffic is august out there."* —*n*. **2**. The peak of the SILLY SEASON, when CIDIOTS, DAY TIPPERS, and WEEKEND WARRIORS reach critical mass, making it all but impossible to perform such routine tasks as grocery shopping, going to the Post Office, etc.

auto compensation *n*. The propensity of an expensive vehicle to expose the stupidity of its owner. *A Range Rover window-deep in ocean surf;*

an exotic sports car that has been stopped by the police or abandoned in the middle of a muddy potato field. Also **revenge effect**.

avant-tarde (a'·vant tard') *n*. **1**. A pioneer of idiocy. **2**. A follower of the latest fashion trends and styles. See **fadget**. —*adj*. **3**. Adorned or equipped with the latest cutting-edge style goods. [FRENCH **avant** (advance), LATIN **tardus** (stupid)] Antonym **avant-garde**.

aw shucks *n*. An affected style of dress intended to demonstrate a modest lifestyle or limited economic means, invariably betrayed by a conspicuously worn 18 carat gold Rolex Oyster Perpetual or Chopard Tourbillion watch, one-half pound gold bracelet or other symbol of immodesty. *e.g., A person wearing Lee overalls and driving a BMW 760*. See **stunting**.

awvenue (aw'·ven·yoo) *n*. **1**. An estate of truly astounding expense, proportion or (rare) quality. **2**. Part of a swank address. *"We have a* COT-TAGE *on Ocean Awvenue."*

babysitter *n.* A person specializing in customer service or customer relations, such as the maître d' in a trendy restaurant.

back roads *n.* A convoluted route through formerly scenic and bucolic neighborhoods that is gridlocked due to its use as an alternate highway in a futile attempt to avoid traffic.

ballet of service *n.* The perfectly timed and choreographed coordination of an extensive team of personal servants at a dinner party or other social function.

BANANA *Acronym.* **Build Absolutely Nothing Anywhere Near Anyone** *n.* A person who has taken an extreme preservationist position in response to the destruction of the essence and character of their community from rampant commercial and residential overdevelopment.

banana peeler *n.* A personal assistant.

barkscaping *adj.* **1.** Excessive use of wood mulch. —*n.* **2.** Spec house landscaping. See **cheapscape**. Antonym (see) **instant forest**.

barnacle *n.* An older man who hangs out in bars, restaurants or nightclubs frequented by young people.

basking shark *n.* **1.** A woman fishing for a rich husband, often through an overt display of sexuality that is intended to provoke a feeding frenzy. **2.** A lawyer on holiday.

bay lice *n.* Jet skis. Also **sea lice**, **lake lice**.

bayfront *adj., n.* Real estate located on a bay and subject to erosion and the incessant buzz of jet skis and motor cruisers. *The second highest valued property type on the* EAST END.

beach, the *n.* **1.** The Hamptons. **2.** The illusion of paradise. **3.** An overcrowded, limited-access public recreation area that is often littered with debris. See **landmines**. **4.** *Obsolete.* The reason for having a vacation house in the Hamptons.

beached *adj. Surfing.* Stuffed to the gills with food.

barnacle

beater *n.* **1**. A crappy car, such as a Range Rover or BMW, that is used specifically for basic transportation in order to protect the condition and value of one's nice car, such as a Bugatti Veyron, Koenigsegg CCX, Ferrari Enzo, Saleen Twin Turbo, Barrett-Jackson 1954 Oldsmobile F-88, etc. **2**. *Surfing.* An often rusty, well-used and much loved vehicle that smells of salt and mold from regular exposure to wet, sandy surf gear.

beaverage *n.* Similar to cleaverage, but utilizing a different part of one's anatomy. *Masculine.* **plumber's crack.** See **cleaverage**.

bed hopping *n.* The practice of availing oneself of any available bed in a share house, preferably one that is already occupied by a member of the opposite sex. See **share house**.

beggar's waltz *n.* An involuntary and often impromptu form of theater, performed on demand and often without rehearsal, usually in an effort to get paid for work that one has completed. See **Jaffe's First Law**.

big *adj.* Vulgar. *"Look at that big house."*

big dog *n.* A person with a net worth of at least $100 million, a brand-name art collection and an interest in a socially acceptable cultural pursuit such as polo, collecting vintage race cars or maintaining a winery.

big house *n*. **1**. A McMansion or megacottage. **2**. A prison.

billing by the pound See **paper the file**.

black book *n*. A record, often maintained by restaurant staff, of people who have broken reservations without notice. Also **black list.** See **reservation redundancy.**

Black Card *n*. **1**. A black American Express Card, originally offered by invitation only to members who charged more than $250,000 per year on their existing platinum accounts. **2**. A device that enables one to instantly get a table at any restaurant, no matter how overbooked. **3**. One of the few blacks ever seen at Nick and Toni's or the Maidstone, Atlantic, Sebonack or Shinnecock Golf Clubs. Also **Centurion Card.**

black helicopter moment *n*. An overwhelming and fear inducing display of power. *e.g., A real estate closing where the buyer pays for a multi-million dollar property with a personal check.*

blank chick *n*. **1**. A pretty but stupid young woman who will do anything. **2**. A fashion model. **3**. A boy's toy. **4**. Ego fodder. *Masculine.* **blank Chuck.**

blockbuster *n*. A deal-breaking offer made on real estate that is already under contract for sale.

blood money *n*. Money earned through actual work, especially if it involves physical labor.

blue chipper *n*. A person of substantial wealth who negotiates the purchase of even the least expensive items.

blue room See **green room.**

BMW *Acronym.* **Bavarian Manure Wagon**. Also **Break My Window**.

board certified specialist *n*. **1**. An ace carpenter. **2**. A talented and experienced surfer.

boat people *pl. n*. Generally elderly DAY TRIP-PERS who travel via ferry to Sag Harbor, commonly identified by their imitation marine apparel and a propensity for ice-cream cones.

bobo *Abbr.* **bourgeois bohemian** *n*. A person who futilely attempts to combine 1960's ideal-

ism with the crass materialism of the 1980's. *e.g.,*
An Earth Day bumper sticker on a Hummer.

Bonac burger (bahn'·ack) *n*. **1**. A sandwich consisting of peanut butter and butter on a stale Kaiser roll. **2**. A young girl. Also **bubby burger** *or* **choker.**

Bonac tonic *n*. Beer.

Bonacker *n*. **1**. An often inbred native of East Hampton who can trace their local lineage back at least three generations. **2**. One who was born on a kitchen table in Springs. **3**. A hillbilly. See **bubby**. *Origin: Name for early settlers of Acabonac Creek, East Hampton.*

boob job *n*. **1**. Something stupidly or poorly done. *A job done by a boob.* **2**. A rite of passage for young women aspiring to high society or a career in the porn industry.

boondoggle *n*. Any construction project in the Hamptons. Conflation of **boonies** (the country) and **dog** (a bad investment). See **Midas touch**.

booty call *n*. A telephone call inadvertently made by sitting on one's cell phone.

boron *n.* **1.** One who talks incessantly about oneself. Conflation of **boring** and **moron**. **boronic** —*adj.* **2.** Relentlessly boring.

bottom feeder *n.* A real estate shopper, speculator or developer who only makes LOWBALL offers on properties where the seller is believed to be desperate.

Boyzilian *n.* The male version of Brazilian bikini waxing.

bozo explosion *n.* See **freak show.**

brand name dropping *v.* Attempting to impress others by casually but frequently mentioning the brand names of goods that one owns. **brand name dropper** —*adj.* See **cost dropping.**

bratitude *n.* The attitude of people who have recently acquired money or children that have never known discipline. *The seven-year-old boy at the former Hampton Day School who bragged to his classmates that his daddy could fire anyone who worked there.*

Bridgehampton *n.* **1.** The Hampton that connects East Hampton to Southampton. **2.** A small hamlet on the East End of Long Island comprised exclusively of real estate offices, restaurants and antique stores. See **hamlet**. **3**. *Obsolete.* A farming community known for potatoes.

Bridgehampton Botanical Gardens *Euphemism*. Marders mega-nursery, where fully mature exotic foliage is available year round. See **instant forest**.

Bridgehamptonization *n*. The transformation of a rural farming community through the teardown and replacement of indigenous architecture with colossal NEOCLASSICAL style spec and vacation houses and massive commercial developments. *Origin: The North Fork of Long island, where residents are terrified that this will happen to their beautiful farms and villages*. See **there goes the neighborhood**.

BriHa (bree'·hah) *abbr.* Verbal shorthand for Bridgehampton that effectively communicates a faddish yet feigned familiarity with the area. *Often pronounced with extra emphasis on the first syllable in the same manner as the classic cinematic cowboy whoop "Yeee-Haa". "I'm going to BRIHA for the weekend!"* See **SoHa, EaHa**.

broke *adj*. **1.** Inadvertently without pocket cash or credit cards. *e.g., Having forgotten one's wallet.* See **flat broke. broker** —*n*. **2.** A person whose job is to expedite the parting of a fool and his money.

brownfield *n*. A tract of previously developed or contaminated land; a premier site for development. *e.g., The radium-contaminated Bulova factory in Sag Harbor, scheduled to be turned into luxury condominiums.* Antonym (see) **greenfield**.

brownie *n*. **1**. An utterly useless seasonal traffic control officer whose only authority is to issue parking tickets. **2**. A police trainee.

bub, bubby *n*. **1**. *Translation from Bonac.* Brother. *"You ain't no bubby unless some bubby loves you."* **2**. A native of East Hampton. **3**. *Obsolete.* A native East Hampton fisherman or clam digger.

bungalow *n*. A diminutive term for one's McMANSION or POCKET ESTATE in the Hamptons. *"We have a bungalow on the beach in East Hampton."* Also **cottage**. See **megacottage.**

buyer blur *n*. The feeling of numbness induced by looking at too many vacation properties listed for sale. *"Was that the one with the view of Ira Rennert's driveway or the one with the fountain in the hot tub?"*

BWI (bee'·we) *Acronym*. **Boating While Intoxicated**. —*n*. A behavior often characterized by attempting to navigate a large motor cruiser from the map printed on a restaurant placemat.

C

Caldor East *n.* **1**. The portion of the East Hampton Town Dump where scavenging is permissible. **2**. Any yard sale primarily supplied by materials reclaimed from the dump. *Origin*: *The former Caldor discount retail center in Bridgehampton*.

campers *n.* People who hang out in trendy restaurants long after finishing their meals, loathe to give up their place in the scene. *"Spill something on those campers at fourteen, we really need the table."* Also **fixtures**. See **scene whore**.

Can you top this? *n.* A social game of conspicuous consumption played among aspiring MASTERS OF THE UNIVERSE for STATUS POINTS.

candy store *n.* The Southampton Town Zoning Board of Appeals, where 95% of variance applications are granted, more than a few out of fear of lawsuits based upon previously granted precedent setting ZBA decisions. *The ZBA defines "hardship' as the Southampton Town Zoning Code.* Also **rubber stamp**. See **Stop & Shop**.

car maid *n.* An automobile detailer, especially one who is retained on a weekly basis.

cashcade (kash·kayd) *n.* **1**. A large income independent of employment, such as a trust fund. **2**. An unstoppable waterfall of money.

cashtaway *n.* A wealthy single person living alone in a huge house; a rich hermit. See **big house**.

cashtipation *n.* The inability to spend or otherwise let go of money. **cashtipated** —*adj.*

cashtration *n.* **1**. Loss of one's money or assets due to external forces, even when such forces have been set into motion by one's own actions. **2**. The intent or effect of a divorce. **cashtrate** —*v.* **3**. To punish economically. **cashtrated** —*adj.*

catch and release *Expression.* See **tag and release**.

cattle car *n.* A bus for CIDIOTS.

cashtaway

cave dweller *n*. **1**. The inhabitant of an apartment in New York City. **2**. A city hick. See **cidiot**.

celebutante *n*. An amateur celebrity. *e.g., Paris Hilton*. Conflation of **celebrity** and **dilettante**.

celebutard *n*. One who is renowned more for their stupidity than their talent. *e.g. Lindsey Lohan*. Conflation of **celebrity** and **retard**.

cellibate *adj*. The state or condition of being without a cell phone.

centimillionaire *adj*. Having a net worth of at least one hundred million but less than one billion dollars. Also **big dog**.

centsless *adj*. **1**. Penny wise and pound foolish. *Negotiating the price of a service so aggressively that one is assured of a cut-rate result*. See **cheese**. **2**. Without pocket change. *e.g., One who uses the tip jar or penny dish at a retail checkout to pay for their purchase*.

certificate of genius *n*. A demonstrated ability to make money. See **gift of God**.

charity ball *n*. A photo op.

charity charade *n*. **1**. A highly profitable event staged by a non-profit organization that distributes negligible sums to the beneficiaries. *e.g., The* HAMPTON CLASSIC, *which despite a budget over $3.5 million, 60,000 spectators and fifty exclusive vendors including Fendi, Hermès of Paris, Jaguar, Land Rover, etc., only donated $40,000 to Southampton Hospital.* **2**. The practice of making contributions to organizations and institutions that are controlled by one's family or that will directly benefit one's personal or business interests. *e.g., Receiving a substantial tax reduction for the donation of a parcel of land to the Nature Conservancy while maintaining full use of the property.* **3**. Make a donation to a charity event solely for publicity purposes. See **charity ball**.

charred sale *n*. A yard sale at which the owner's furnishings are sold by the tenants at the end of the summer rental.

cheapscape *n*. **1**. The minimally landscaped site around a brand new house. *Often the result of blowing one's budget on the construction of a* McMANSION. **2**. Spec house landscaping. Antonym **instant forest**. See **barkscaping**.

checkbook environmentalist *n*. One who writes a check in the amount of a few thousand dollars to an organization such as the Nature Conservancy while on a personal jet commute to one of their many vacation estates, where acres of lawn are immaculately maintained through the generous use of irrigation systems, pesticides, fungicides and chemical fertilizers, the outdoor swimming pool is kept heated to body temperature through November and both the 12,000 square foot main house and the 3,800 square foot guest cottage are maintained at a constant 68 degrees year-round, despite the fact that the property is only used a few weekends each year. See **exemptionalist**.

cheep *n*. The sound produced when a tightwad walks.

cheese *v*. **1**. To place additional demands or requirements after negotiating the terms of a deal. *e.g., Agree on a purchase price for a house, then demand that the furniture be included in the deal, or that the price be reduced for various minor defects noted in an engineer's report.* [LATIN **caseus**, from PROTO-INDO-EUROPEAN base **kwat** (to sour)] **cheeser** —*adj*. **2**. One who cheeses or practices cheesing. See **it's a deal**.

Chevy subdivision *n*. An SUV that is larger than a house. See **wheel estate.**

chictionary *n.* A man's black book of women's telephone numbers.

choker See **Bonac burger**.

chowder *Surfing. n.* Water pollution; floating debris such as such as human waste, hurricane wreckage, etc. *"The break looks sweet, but it's full of chowder."* See **Neptune cocktail**.

Chubby Checker *Surfing. n.* A type of poser, typically a middle-aged, heavyset male who spends a primo surf day checking all the best spots, chatting about conditions, but who never actually paddles out. Chubby Checkers loiter conspicuously in the parking lot before declaring the surf isn't perfect enough and moving on. *"This sucks, I'm going to DITCH."* See **poser**.

chum slick *n.* A group of boisterous young men often seen hanging out in nightclubs and bars aggressively trying to pick up young ladies. *Chum slicks are characterized by loud, rowdy behavior and the liberal use of lame pick-up lines.* See **555**.

cidiot (city·it) *Literal* "an idiot from the city." *n.* **1**. A person who does not know how to behave when removed from their natural urban environment. *A city hick*. **2**. An urban cave dweller who, while traveling or vacationing in the country, behaves without consideration for local custom or rules. *"There's a cidiot parked in the fire zone."* **3**. A philistine with delusions of grandeur. *Arrogant public display of superiority is one of the key qualities of cidiocy.* **cidiocy** —*adj.* **4**. The self-delusion of being savvy. Conflation of **city** and **idiot**.

circling *n*. A pre-mating behavior, often performed in nightclubs, in which two people circle each other for inspection, similar to the manner in which dogs meet. See **cold cuts**.

cleaverage *n*. Cleavage that is used by a woman as leverage to get a man to do something she wants. *e.g., Victoria used her cleaverage to get a free pass to the STAR ROOM.*

cloak *v*. **1**. Keep a low profile. **2**. Stay close to home; avoiding driving, shopping, etc. Also **ghost**. —*n*. **3**. The preferred behavior of locals during the SILLY SEASON, especially on weekends and holidays. **cloaked** —*adj.*

clocksucker *n*. A person who drags out a job or project in order to drive up the cost. See **construction screw**.

Club Fed *n.* A State sponsored vacation home for Hamptons' notables such as Martha Stewart (*insider trading*), Lizzie Grubman (*vehicular assault*), Daniel Pelosi (*murder*), ImClone CEO Sam Waksal (*insider trading and fraud*), Arnold Bengis (*international poaching and smuggling*), etc.

cold cuts *pl. n.* Patrons at singles bar. See **slaughterhouse.**

cold war *n.* Competitive conspicuous consumption; the ongoing struggle to outspend one's social adversaries. *Upgrading from a $8,500 Sub-Zero refrigerator to a $12,500 Northland Master Series, or better yet, to an even more expensive out-of production Traulson commercial refrigerator with glass doors, which requires staff to keep the visible interior clean and organized.*

command performance *n.* A public blunder made while attempting to display wealth and power. *Accidentally setting off the alarm in one's $100,000 automobile directly in front of the crowd seated at a trendy outdoor café.* See **James Blonde.**

compass *n.* **1.** A personal security detail. **compassed** —*adj.* **2.** Protected by a personal security detail. *Having bodyguards stationed at three, six, nine and twelve o'clock. Derivation:* **encompassed.**

compensatory enrichment *n.* Lavish gifts given, especially to one's children, as a substitute for love and attention. See **Lizzie Grubman Effect**.

confirmed bachelor *Euphemism.* Flaming homosexual.

conspicuous consumption *n.* A highly visible flag with which to attract salesmen, thieves, kidnappers, con men, fund raisers, environmental activists, social satirists, etc.

construction manager *n.* A general contractor in disguise. See **general contractor.**

construction screw *n.* A poorly trained, unprofessional or otherwise incompetent tradesman or subcontractor. *A worker who arrives late or fails to show up entirely, overcharges, steals building materials, does poor quality work, sleeps on the job, etc.*

consumption *n.* A highly infectious disease characterized by lesions on one's bank account and massive accumulation of material goods, particularly those of high cost which are rarely, if ever, used. Also **white plague**.

contemporary *adj., n.* An architectural style once common in the Hamptons, best described as modernism after fifty years of PROLETARIAN DRIFT, that signifies nothing other than a complete lack of aesthetic sensibility.

Cook-out *n.* A traditional Hamptons recreational activity in which an older, pedigreed Lothario cheats on his middle-aged yet still beautiful wife with a girl in her teens.

corporate landscape *n.* An area where real estate is predominantly deeded to corporations as tax and liability shelters or to hide the identity of the real owners. See **hedge fund**.

corporate landscaper *n.* A guy with a lawn mower, pickup truck and glossy multi-page color brochure offering a suite of landscape services from grass cutting, edging, and fertilization to irrigation, pesticides, fungicides, herbicides, hedge trimming, tree pruning, etc.

cost drop *v.* **1.** Disclose the cost of a product or service one has purchased, either to impress others with one's ability to make such stupendous expenditures or to astound others with one's cheapness. —*n.* **2.** A competitive version of "can you top this" played between self-appointed MASTERS OF THE UNIVERSE for STATUS

POINTS. **cost dropper** —*n.* **3.** One who attempts to impress others by referring to the cost of goods and services they have purchased, especially in a complaining way, as if unable to afford them. *"The tuition for Madison's preschool is $34,000."*

cottage *n.* Diminutive term for one's McMANSION in the Hamptons. *"We have a cottage on the beach in East Hampton."* See **megacottage**.

counter monkey *n.* A person who is assumed to be poor and ignorant because they work behind the counter in a retail establishment, and is treated accordingly. See **degradation ceremony**.

country, the *Euphemism.* Suburbia.

cranial-rectal inversion *n.* A severe psychophysiological condition for which CASHTRATION is the only reliable cure. See **MOTUS.**

craptacular *adj.* Spectacularly awful, especially if at great financial cost.

creeping Hamptonism *n.* Rude behavior visited upon those who live outside of the Hamptons by those on their way to the Hamptons.

e.g., An FUV parked in the Fire Zone at the King Kullen supermarket in Manorville.

crying poor *n*. **1**. Wealthy people who complain that they don't have any money. See **relative deprivation**. **2**. People who live in the Hamptons in a house that they own but who don't own any other property. See **marginally rich**.

cultural guide *n*. Any publication used to identify products safe for consumption by social climbers. *e.g., The New York Times, Hamptons Magazine, New York Magazine, etc.* See **sheeple**.

curb appeal *n*. The first impression of a house or a hooker as seen from the street.

curtesy *n*. Insincere or outright mocking courtesy. *e.g., To say "good day" instead of "hello".* **curteous** —*adj.*

cusstomer *n*. An ill-behaved or foul-mouthed patron. *A customer who uses foul language or whose behavior inspires the use of foul language by others.*

custom *adj*. **1**. Amazingly or expensively screwed up. *"We're building a custom house in Southampton."* **2**. Broken. Also **customized.**

CWD *Acronym.* **Celebrity Worship Disorder** *n.* An obsessive and often prurient interest in celebrities. *"If we go to Nick and Tony's we might see Jerry Seinfeld!"*

Dan's Papers *n.* An AD RAG and social guide for CIDIOTS.

day of the dead *n.* An open house for real estate brokers.

day tripper *n.* A tourist who returns home for the night. See **poorist.**

deck candy *n.* Attractive girls in bikinis hanging around swimming pools or on boats.

deck change *n.* The act of changing into or out of a bathing suit under a towel.

deconstructivism *n.* An architectural style that passes for avant-garde among FADGETS and the hopelessly ignorant.

deli case with cold cuts

decorator *n.* A person hired to provide one with the perceived accessories of the social class to which one aspires. Conflation of **décor** (stage setting) and **tor** (a rocky hilltop).

decorator dog See **designer dog.**

degradation ceremony *n.* An important part of class interaction in society, in which lower classes are labeled as inferior and subjected to humiliation. *e.g., Verbally abusing store clerks, waiters, personal staff, employees and others as a demonstration of one's wealth, power and social status.* See **mobile.**

deli case *n.* A singles bar, nightclub or other place or event where getting laid is the primary objective. See **cold cuts**.

delocate *v.* Market a property as if it were situated in a more expensive, attractive or desirable area than it actually is. *e.g., Advertising a property off Steven Hands Path as being located in far more prestigious Georgica.* **delocated** —*adj.* [LATIN **de-** (from, off, apart, away), **locare**, **locat-**, (to place)]

derrick *n.* A hot guy. *"Look at that derrick over by the pool."*

designer babble *n.* Incomprehensible explanation, often utilizing baroque and byzantine language, used to justify plans, specifications, work authorizations and purchase orders made by architects and INFERIOR DECORATORS. See **talkitecture**.

designer dog *n.* A custom breed of canine, often the result of an unintended pairing, adopted as a status symbol. *A Labradoodle, Cockapoo, Huskador, German Sheagle, etc.* Also **decorator dog**.

destitute *adj.* Having a net worth of less than one million dollars. See **broke**.

destructions *n.* **1.** Plans for the construction of a MEGACOTTAGE or other trophy structure that will destroy a large swath of the natural environment. **2.** Any set of plans, drawings or specifications that result in a debacle. Also **enginerring**.

developer See **philandrapist**.

dinner theater *n.* A couple having a major fight in a swank restaurant.

dirty rich *adj.* **1.** Less than filthy rich. **2.** A self-deprecating expression often used by the filthy rich, seemingly to disparage their wealth but actually to celebrate it. *"I'm not filthy rich, I'm just dirty rich."* See **filthy rich.**

disposable fashion *n.* Clothes worn once and thrown away. *e.g., Ivana Trump's wardrobe.* Also **casht-offs.**

disturbia *n.* A very wealthy and invariably highly neurotic suburban community. *e.g., The Hamptons, Beverly Hills, Greenwich, etc.* **disturban** *—adj.* See **neurodiversity.**

Ditch *n.* Ditch Plains, a tiny, often overcrowded surf spot in Montauk, notable primarily for the number of collisions between surfers. See **Chubby Checker.**

diversity *n.* An educational concept, usually encountered in an exclusive setting such as the now defunct Morriss Center Hampton Day School, that teaches the necessity of occasionally having to deal with those who are less entitled than oneself.

divine *adj.* Expensively showy. See **sacrilegious.**

Do you know who I am? *Expression.* A question foreshadowing a temper tantrum by a self-appointed MASTER OF THE UNIVERSE whose expectations have been frustrated.

Do you take cash? *Expression.* A question foretelling an attempt to negotiate the price of an item or service or to avoid paying sales tax, used exclusively by those who can well afford both the price and the tax. See **mize**.

dog that caught the car *Expression.* A person who has reached their goal but doesn't know what to do next. *e.g., People who have purchased vacation houses in the Hamptons but don't know what to do with themselves when there.* See **parvenu**.

doorstop *n.* A bound stack of AD RAGS, fresh from the publisher, ready to be delivered to the landfill. See **Dan's Papers.**

downtown *n.* A term used by CIDIOTS to describe any small village or hamlet center in the Hamptons, often consisting of only a single main street, as if it were a thriving metropolis. *"I'm going downtown to the Candy Kitchen."* Antonym **uptown**. See **town**.

drain surgeon *n.* An excellent or very expensive plumber, especially one that requires an appointment several months in advance.

dream house *Expression*. A term used exclusively by real estate speculators to gain sympathy, favor, reduced construction rates, no-cost extras, etc. from workers and contractors on a construction project that will invariably be sold immediately upon completion. *"I love it - it's my dream house!"* See **philandrapist**.

dressing down *v.* **1**. Projecting an air of self-importance by lecturing, criticizing or berating one's staff, pointedly within the hearing distance of others, especially over a cell phone, which may or may not be turned on. See **degradation ceremony**. **2**. Projecting an air of self-importance by dressing below what is expected for an event, implying that urgent critical matters precluded one's ability to don proper attire or that the event did not merit one's best appearance. —*n*. **3**. A visual or vocal component of urgent haste. See **urgent haste.**

dumpster diving *v.* **1**. Rummaging through a trash container for useful or salable items. See **Caldor East**. **2**. Searching through discarded material in search of otherwise unattainable information such as credit card and bank account numbers, passwords, the identity of a TRASHOLE, etc. **dumpster diver** —*n*. See **trashole**.

EaHa (ee'·hah) *abbr.* Verbal shorthand for East Hampton that effectively communicates a faddish yet feigned familiarity with the area. *Often pronounced with extra emphasis on the first syllable in the same manner as the classic cinematic cowboy whoop "Yeee-Haa'.* See **BriHa, SoHa.**

East End, the *n.* Vernacular term for the geographic area extending from the Shinnecock Canal eastward to Montauk Point, location of the most expensive real estate in the United States. See **the Hamptons**.

East Hampton Village *n.* **1.** A resort community formerly named *"America's most beautiful village"*, now exclusively populated with UPSCALE international chain stores and aggressively over-patrolled by rabid local police. **2.** A place where the rent on commercial property makes Fifth Avenue in Manhattan look like a bargain.

east of the canal *n.* **1**. That portion of Long Island geographically defined as being east of the Shinnecock Canal. See **The East End.** —*adj.* **2**. Expensive; characterized by the high prices typical of the Hamptons. **3**. Exclusive, but only from an economic point of view. **4**. Geographically desirable. Antonym **west of the canal.**

eavesdrop *n.* A structural condition endemic to SPEC HOUSES and McMANSIONS. *The inevitable result of houses built hurriedly with shortcuts including the cheapest available materials and labor.*

ecologist *adj.* A person with a higher than normal concern for the environment. *e.g., The man who, not wanting to put the existing house on his newly purchased dream lot in East Hampton into the landfill, bought the land next door to move the structure to so that he could build his DREAM HOUSE on the first lot, then bought and renovated another house across the street to live in while the other work was being done.* See **environmentalist**.

economically challenged *adj.* **1**. Unable to afford a vacation house in the Hamptons. *e.g., The millionaire who, unable to afford even the cheapest property for sale, slunk out of the Hamptons real estate office with his tail between his legs.* **2**. Barely able to afford to live in the Hamptons. *A local* *person or family who, despite working multiple jobs, is on the verge of being financially squeezed out of their home in the Hamptons because of the exorbitant cost of living there.* See **Hamptons shuffle**.

economy class syndrome *n.* **1**. A debilitating condition characterized by the inability to pay full or even fair price for any purchase. **2**. The tendency of a wealthy person to aggressively negotiate the cost of all goods and services. See **blue chipper**.

egotheism *n.* The deification of oneself. *Egotheism is most notably exemplified by the construction of monuments to one's self. Such monuments are located not in places of grandeur, but in crowded neighborhoods full of similar monuments such as Further Lane in East Hampton, Meadow Lane in Southampton, Green River Cemetery in Springs, etc.* See **master of the universe**.

emotional detonation *n.* A sudden, spontaneous and often unanticipated verbal and or physical explosion triggered by severe mental anguish or physical discomfort. *Emotional detonations are usually ignited by grave impediments to one's lifestyle such as discovering that the restaurant is out of avocados, being unable to find a parking* *space, having to wait more than ten seconds for ser-vice, etc.*

End, the *n*. Montauk.

enginerring See **destructions**.

entitlement *n*. The attitude and behavior, justified by wealth, that the world and all its bounties belong to one by right. See **privilege**.

entourrage (on·toor·rage') *n*. **1**. Riotous or undisciplined behavior by members of one's entourage, such as fighting in a bar or nightclub. **2**. Anger over the bad publicity caused by the misbehavior of one's entourage.

entry-lux *adj*. Low-priced luxury-brand goods designed to appeal to a broader economic mar-ket. *e.g., BMW 3-series, Land Rover LR3, Jaguar S-Type, etc.*

environmentalist *n*. One who writes a check in the amount of a few thousand dollars to an organization such as the Nature Conservancy while on personal jet commute to one of their many vacation estates, where acres of lawn are immaculately maintained through the generous use of irrigation systems, pesticides, fungicides and chemical fertilizers, the outdoor swimming pool is kept heated to body temperature through November and both the 12,000 square foot main house and the 3,800 square foot guest cottage are maintained at a constant 68 degrees year-round, despite the fact that the property is only used a few weekends each year. See **exemptionalist**.

estate *n*. **1**. *Real Estate*. A cluster of buildings on a single large property that includes, at the very least; separate family, guest and servant's quarters, maintenance and storage facilities, formal gardens, recreational facilities such as stables and an industrialized agricultural activity such as a vineyard. —*adj*. **2**. A property so large that its primary structure is not visible from any public road or neighboring property. **3**. A property so large that its full extent cannot be seen or even guessed at from the view available from any structure on the property. —*n*. **4**. *Obsolete*. A tract of land with hereditary rights granted by royal charter. **5**. A castle or manor and the surrounding feudal lands. **6**. *British*. A housing development. **7**. *Law*. The things that one's relatives fight over after one has died.

estate manager See **pest control device**.

estate security *n.* The practice of replacing all of the personnel employed at one's estate on a regular basis, such as once a year, specifically to avoid having to give them a raise.

esteemed *adj.* The emotional state of a wealthy person forced to wait. *e.g., A MASTER OF THE UNIVERSE waiting for service at a busy restaurant.* See **timed-out**.

ethical deficit *n.* The amount by which another person's principles or behavior falls short of one's own.

ethical surplus *n.* The amount by which another person's principles or behavior exceeds one's own.

ethical void *n.* The real estate market in the Hamptons. *Those who believe that money will do anything will do anything for money.*

Euro *n.* An afro for Caucasians, usually worn in a vain attempt to appear stylish, often see on EUROBES or EUROTRASH SLUMMING in the Hamptons.

Eurobe (u·ro'·bee) *n.* A EUROTRASH wannabe.

Euro

Eurotrash *adj., n.* European pseudo-sophisticates living or vacationing in trendy U.S. resorts. *"Ach, you Americans, you are so primitive."* See **slumming**.

excessible *adj.* Capable of being expanded or enhanced beyond reason or prudence. Also **easy excess**. Antonym **maxed out**. See **addition**.

exemptionalist *n.* One who believes, because of their great financial wealth, that they are exempt from the accepted laws and socially responsible behaviors that govern society.

expiration dating *n.* Romance defined as temporary from the onset. *A Hamptons summer romance.* See **bed hopping**.

faddict *n.* One who obsessively follows all of the latest trends and fads in fashion, technology and travel. Faddicts are readily identified by chrome wheel spinners on an SUV, trips to the latest *Condé Nast Traveler* hotspot, a Krups Panini Press, GPS enabled Blackberry, etc. Also **fadget**.

fake and bake *n.* A tanning salon. See **instant tan.**

fake entrepreneur *adj.* A person who was born on third base and thinks they've hit a home run. See **hit the daily double.**

False Authority Syndrome *n.* The tendency to assume that a person of financial wealth also has refined behavior, higher education, a sophisticated palate, social consciousness, depth of knowledge or expertise in at least one field, etc. *False Authority Syndrome can take any of several forms ranging from self-delusion to mass hysteria.*

fantasy *n*. **1**. The ability to dream, the measure of which is inversely proportional to the amount of one's liquid wealth. *When a person can afford to buy anything they want, there is nothing left to dream about except how fast they can acquire it, thus the necessity of the wealthy to have instantaneous service.* **2**. The stuff that dreams are made of. *"I'm having a 1963 Ferrari 400 Superamerica delivered Thursday. I expect you to build me a climate-controlled four-car garage by then."* See **timed-out**.

farble *n*. Faux marble.

farm stand *n*. **1**. The last vestige of once thriving and widespread local agriculture. **2**. A roadside tourist trap. *"Pumpkins? They're $7 a pound."*

Farmer's Law *Adage*. "Anything with tits or wheels is nothing but trouble."

fashmere *n*. Faux cashmere. Also **trashmere**. See **Salvation Armani**.

fasod (fa·sahd´) *n*. An attempt to act sober while totally bombed. *"Just take the keys; don't fall for Billy's fasod."* Variation of **facade**.

fat choice *n.* **1**. Selecting one's next opulent expenditure, *"I can't decide between the king-size Mink bedspread or the Chinchilla one. I guess I'll just have to get both."* **2**. The options usually available at a SIDEWALK SALE.

featuritis *n.* A consumptive disease characterized by the tendency to add every conceivable option, no matter how frivolous, useless or expensive, to one's purchases.

Feng Shui (fung' shway) *n.* **1**. The ancient Chinese art or practice of positioning graves. **2**. A marketing technique commonly used to sell high-profit and otherwise unsaleable objects to socially insecure people who are not Chinese. See **inferior decoration.**

fifty footer *n.* A person who looks attractive from a distance due to an extreme effort to maintain their appearance or the failing eyesight of the observer. See **MDL.**

file cinco *Law Enforcement n.* An unlicensed, unregistered and uninsured motorist. *Formerly* **file five**.

filter factor *n*. The effect of real estate prices and the cost of living on the type of people able to visit, live or own property in the Hamptons.

filthy rich *adj*. **1.** Less than obscenely rich. **2.** A self-deprecating expression often used by the obscenely rich, seemingly to disparage their wealth but actually to celebrate it. *"I'm not obscenely rich, I'm just filthy rich."* See **obscenely rich.**

fire zone *n*. Reserved parking for Range Rovers.

fiscalamity *n*. An economic disaster. *e.g., Being convicted of tax evasion or insider trading, or cleaned out in a divorce.* Also **cashtastrophe.**

555 *v*. Give a bogus telephone number to a pickup con artist. *"555 that jerk and let's get out of here."*

flat broke *adj*. Having a net worth of less than $10 million. See **penniless.**

flatinum *n*. Fake jewelry. Also **blang.** Antonym **bling.** See **noisy jewelry.**

flip *v.* **1**. Purchase a piece of property and then immediately resell it for a profit. **flipper** —*n*. **2**. A real estate day trader.

foak *n.* Faux oak. *e.g., Formica.*

foreploy *n.* A mistruth or fabrication about oneself told with the intent of convincing another to have sex or enter into a business deal. *"I'm a partner at Goldman Sachs."*

Fourbucks *n.* Starbucks, where "tall" is tiny and a cup of coffee is both smaller and considerably more expensive than anywhere else. *Proof that a fool and his money are soon parted.*

four footer *n.* An illegal immigrant, especially one working as a day laborer. See **labor tourist.**

franchise terrorism *n.* The indiscriminate placing of franchise and chain stores, such as the Starbucks in Bridgehampton, without consideration or respect for the surrounding community.

franite *n.* Faux granite. *e.g., Corian.*

Frankenhouse See **monster house**.

freak show

freak show *n.* **1**. An outlandishly or inappropriately dressed person. *Ralph Lauren wearing a duck hunting outfit to the Candy Kitchen, pretending to be a local.* **2**. Any Hamptons Main Street during the SILLY SEASON, even more so on a Friday or weekend, especially at night. **3**. The payload of a tourist bomb. See **tourist bomb**. Also **bozo explosion**.

free rider *n.* A wealthy person who attends a fund raiser for free. *e.g., Arranging to see a Hamptons Designer Show House through a real estate broker rather than making the $30 per person donation to Southampton Hospital.*

freeboater *adj., n.* **1**. One who pirates accommodations on board a ship headed to or moored in Sag Harbor, Conscience Point, Three Mile Harbor, etc. **2**. A yachting groupie.

fresh meat *n.* New arrivals in the Hamptons. *Easy prey for unscrupulous real estate brokers, attorneys, general contractors, restaurant proprietors, landscapers, etc.*

fresh out's *n.* Thayer's Hardware in Bridgehampton, where the last of whatever one was looking for was sold just a moment ago.

frozen asset *n.* One's face after a botox treatment.

FUV *Acronym.* **Fuck You Vehicle** *n.* **1.** Any extraordinarily large, exotic or expensive SUV. *e.g., A Hummer, Lamborghini LM002, Mercedes-Benz G Series, Range Rover, Porsche Cayenne, Lexus LX, etc.* **2.** The WEEKEND WARRIOR'S vehicle of choice.

Garage Mahal *n.* An ornately designed and detailed oversize residential garage with a minimum capacity of four automobiles, typically equipped with imported stone floor, custom stainless steel workbenches with exotic wood cabinetry, fully loaded Snap-on Master Series rolling tool cabinets, washroom, refrigerated storage, integrated audio-video systems, etc.

garmento *n.* **1.** One who made their money in Manhattan's cutthroat garment district and is unable to refrain from unscrupulous chiseling and double dealing in any situation or setting. —*adj.* **2.** Scrupulously disabled. Also **cloakie**.

gazump v. **1.** To refuse to close a sale contract on a house or property because one has received a better offer. *gazumped* —*adj.* **2.** Outbid on a real property. **3.** Cheated out of what should have rightfully belonged to one. [Yiddish **gezumph** (swindle)]

gazunder *v.* Lower one's purchase offer at the last minute, forcing the seller of a house or property to reduce the price accordingly or cancel the deal. See **cheese**.

gelding *n.* A formerly rich man. See **cashtration**.

general contractor *n.* The person at the very top of the construction pyramid scheme.

generosity *n.* Taking less than one can.

gift of God *Expression.* The ability to make lots of money. *If you want to know what God thinks of money, just look at who he gave it to.*

glass house *n.* **1.** A house with zero privacy. **2.** Any fragile construct, such as one's carefully built ego. **3.** *Surfing.* The space inside of a tubular wave. *Where you are when shooting the tube.*

go away money *n.* **1.** A payment made to settle a frivolous legal action simply because it is less expensive than properly defending oneself against it. **2.** A token donation to a charitable cause. *"Here's a dollar. It's all you're going to get. Now, go away."* **3.** Any payment made to rid oneself of a nuisance.

general contractor

go back to Joisey *Expression.* A phrase often hurled at LOCALS by CIDIOTS, especially while driving in the Hamptons.

go native *v.* **1**. Blend into one's surroundings. **2**. Eschew trendy restaurants and parties in favor of quiet dinners at home and other low-key behaviors. See **cloak**.

gold plating *n.* Unnecessary items included in a design or construction project to justify an increase in cost and the fees associated fees with the work. **gold plate** —*v.* **gold plated** —*adj.* See **featuritis**.

golden ghetto *n.* An area with an above average concentration of affluent housing and high-end stores; especially where traditional mom and pop businesses have been replaced by international chain stores such as Coach and Ralph Lauren. *e.g., East Hampton Village.* Also **prosperity blight**.

golden hello *n. Obsolete.* A tip one gives to a maître d', parking attendant, etc. prior to being served.

golden myopia *n.* The inability to perceive the existence of those below one's social rank. *"Did you hear something, darling?"*

Golden Rule, the *Adage.* "Those with the gold make the rules."

goodbye *Interjection.* Used to direct another to leave. Also **get out**. See **curtsey**.

green *n.* The only color that really matters.

Green River Cemetery *n.* An elite cemetery in Springs where all of the 110 remaining six-figure burial plots were purchased by the widow of a wealthy executive. See **egotheism**.

green room *Construction. n.* A portable toilet housed in a green fiberglass enclosure, usually found at construction sites, public events and swank Hamptons parties where the host won't allow guests to use the facilities. Also **Mexican space shuttle**.

greenfield *n.* A tract of as-yet undeveloped land; a premier site for development. *e.g., The scenic and historic farm field at the Bridgehampton Historical Society's Corwith House.* Antonym **brownfield**.

greenwash *n.* The illusion of environmental responsibility. *e.g., A couple of solar electric panels on a 11,000 square foot vacation house.*

grouper *n*. **1**. A tenant in an illegal group rent-al. See **hampster**. **2.** A bottom feeder.

guest *n*. A CIDIOT who, while on vacation, acts as if local residents were STAFF. See **tourist**.

hamlet *n.* **1**. A small community, similar to a village, except without its own municipal government and therefore destined for tragedy. *e.g., Water Mill*. **2**. The realm of Princes. *e.g., Bridgehampton*. **3**. A former Prince of Denmark.

hamp, hampere (ham·pir') *n.* A standard unit of intensity in the International System of Units, equivalent to seeing one celebrity.

hamperage *n.* The magnitude of a Hamptons event as measured in hamps. See **hamp**.

hample *adj.* Beyond ample; more than more than enough. *e.g., His and hers Hummers*.

hamplification *n.* **1**. The glorification of excess. **hamplify** —*v.*

hampster *n.* A small and relatively insignificant rodent, active during the summer months, that leaves a trail of waste and garbage around its burrow and the watering holes it frequents. *e.g., A tenant in a share house in the Hamptons.* Also **grouper**.

hampster cage *n.* A group rental or SHARE HOUSE in the Hamptons.

Hampton Bays *n.* Workforce housing for Hamptons service personnel. Conflation of **Hamptons** and **bay** (storage area or pit). See **west of the canal**.

Hampton Classic *n.* **1.** A story that exemplifies everything that is wrong with the Hamptons. *e.g., The woman who, after waiting weeks for her reservation at Nick and Toni's, calmly finished her dinner after her husband, who had collapsed to the floor, was carted off by paramedics.* **2.** One of the largest manure-producing events in the United States, annually held in a former potato field in Bridgehampton. See **charity charade.**

Hampton Jitney See **cattle car**.

Hampton serenade *n.* The continuous and often overwhelming cacophony of: gasoline powered hedge trimmers, lawn mowers, leaf

Hampton Jitney

blowers, low flying private jets and helicopters, cigarette boats, jet skis, the screaming sirens of emergency vehicles, automobile horns and security alarms, loud music and other noise from restaurants, nightclubs, house parties, etc.

Hamptonectomy *n*. Radical removal from the Hamptons, often self-imposed for medical reasons. See **Hamptonitus**.

Hamptonescent *adj*. **1**. Reminiscent of the Hamptons; like or similar to the Hamptons. **2**. Overly crowded, overly trendy and way too expensive.

Hamptoniac *n*. A person affected with HAMP-TONOSIS.

Hamptonite *adj*. **1**. One who falsely claims residency in the Hamptons. **2**. A person who owns property in the Hamptons but does not live there. **3**. *Law Enforcement*. A self-centered, Mercedes-Benz driving ignoramus. *e.g., A person who stops at the scene of a car accident to ask police for directions.*

Hamptonitus *n*. **1**. Severe, allergic reaction to CIDIOTS. **2**. The deleterious physical, mental, emotional and spiritual condition caused by overexposure to the Hamptons.

Hamptonium *Mythology. n.* **1**. A rare and exceedingly valuable element that bestows supreme social status. *The toniest of all the elements.* **2**. The substance responsible for the high price of Hamptons consumer goods. *e.g., The mysterious ingredient responsible for the $8.00 cost of a single scoop ice cream cone at Dylan's Candy Bar in East Hampton.*

Hamptonization *n.* The transformation of a poor rural community into a heavily trafficked and absurdly expensive DISTURBIA.

Hamptonologist *n.* **1**. A self-styled expert on the Hamptons who is basically clueless. *e.g, Barbara Kopple, executive producer of the television documentary "The Hamptons".* **2**. A writer who has made a career out of exploiting people suffering from HAMPTONOSIS, *e.g., James Brady, Stephen Gaines, etc.*

Hamptonosis *n.* A psychotic condition characterized by obsessive fascination with anything related to the Hamptons.

Hamptons, the *n.* **1**. A brand name resort designated safe for consumption and accumulation of STATUS POINTS by the A-LIST, celebrities and other social authorities. *"I'm going to the Hamptons for the weekend."* **2**. A catchall phrase used to describe the East End of Long Island by those unfamiliar with the area. See **East End**. **3**. A former cluster of small hamlets and villages that has been transformed into an overcrowded, polluted and absurdly expensive suburbia, indistinguishable from other trendy resorts that capitalize on greed, bad taste and the utter lack of both individuality and intelligence. See **Hamptonization**. **4**. A term used to add appeal or allure to a product or service. *The Hamptons Diet*. —*adj*. **5**. Shallow; pretentious; affected. *"I'd go to that party at Martha's if it weren't so Hamptons." Origin: The term "the Hamptons" was first used by Real Estate Broker Allan Schneider, who for marketing purposes, grouped the individual villages and hamlets of the East End together under a single name.* See **Schneidered**.

Hamptons age *n*. The age that fits the persona that one is trying to project. *e.g., The age claimed by an* OVERLOADED *teenager trying to get into a nightclub or a* BARNACLE *trying to get into the pants of a* BLANK CHICK.

Hamptons Magazine *n*. A glossy AD RAG and social guide for the PARVENU that glorifies the lifestyles of the rich and excessive. See **hamplification**.

Hamptons price *n*. The standard price plus anywhere between 15% and 100%. *It's the Hamptons, why pay less?*

Hamptons shuffle, the *n*. **1**. A ritual dance performed exclusively by the working class, the steps of which consist of maintaining multiple jobs, or working double- or triple-time in a single job, in an increasingly futile attempt to be able to afford to live in the Hamptons. **2**. The exhausting weekend commute between one's city residence and vacation house in the Hamptons. See **weekend warrior**.

hamputee *adj*. **1**. One who is cut off while waiting in line at a Hamptons supermarket, restaurant, deli, library, bank or other place of business, or while driving in the Hamptons, by a self-appointed MASTER OF THE UNIVERSE whose time is, of course, far more valuable than one's own. *n*. **2**. The driver, often of a LAND YACHT or FUV, who is either unwilling or unable to signal impending directional changes.

handicap spot *n*. Reserved parking areas for the mentally impaired, who invariably drive FUVs, Mercedes, BMWs, etc. See **disturbia**.

handyman's special *n*. Any real property in less than ideal condition, allegedly priced at a discount. *"I saw a handyman's special in Springs for $895,000."* See **recycle**.

happy look *n.* The perpetual sneer worn by the never satisfied.

harmoneyous *adj.* Agreeably well moneyed.

haught couture (hawt koo·tur') *n.* A scornful, condescendingly proud and aggressively superior style of fashion, often displayed in settings such as the Candy Kitchen in Bridgehampton or Saint Andrew's Dune Church in Southampton. See **freak show**.

haut kitsch *Literal* "high trash." *n.* A style based on transcending the mundane, often implemented inadvertently while attempting to accomplish something quite different. See **inferior decoration**.

hawking *v.* **1.** Slow cruising and circling, in search of either a sexual conquest or a parking spot. **2.** While driving, following a pedestrian in the hope of capturing their parking spot when they leave. Also **vultching**.

hedge fund *n.* **1.** A vacation property in the Hamptons. **2.** The sum of money allocated to the landscaping of new McMANSION or MEGA-COTTAGE. See **instant forest**.

heir pollution *n*. **1**. A large number of heirs and or heiresses concentrated in a small area. **2**. A large number of offspring produced by a wealthy person.

heir pressure *n*. **1**. Demands made by one's potential heirs. See **heirass**. **2**. The stress of having to share an inheritance. See **heir raid**.

heir raid *n*. The actions initiated upon the death of a wealthy parent, spouse or other benefactor, often involving teams of lawyers and private detectives. See **heircraft**.

heirass (aer'·as) *n*. A persistently irritating and ill-behaved heir to great wealth. *e.g., Luke Weil, Paris Hilton*.

heirbrained *adj*. **1**. Consumed by one's potential inheritance. **2**. Mad as a March hare; giddy; foolhardy.

heircraft (aer'·kraft) *n*. **1**. The art of positioning oneself to receive the largest possible inheritance. Also **heirmanship**. **2**. A personal jet or private yacht. Also **heir transport**.

heirhead (aer'·hed) *adj., n.* A person of inherited wealth with far more money than sense. *e.g., Paris Hilton.*

heirlock (aer'·lok) *n.* The condition of being sole beneficiary. *"She has an* HEIRLOCK *on the estate."*

heirsickness *n.* 1. Feelings of nausea, fatigue or annoyance resulting from unceasing whining and constant attempts at manipulation by one's heirs. See **heir pressure**. 2. A debilitating condition affecting potential beneficiaries in line to inherit great wealth, characterized by indolence, impatience, frustration and irritation. 3. A public health hazard caused by overexposure to heirs and heiresses. *e.g., Donald Trump, Paris Hilton, etc.* heirsick —*adj.*

hicnic *n.* A white trash barbecue.

high roller *n.* A person who gets a flat tire and buys a new car.

himbo *n.* An attractive but stupid or shallow man. Variation of **bimbo**. Also **blank chuck**.

hipatitus *n.* Chronic, incurable coolness. See **fadget**.

hiring hall *n.* A job center for illegal immigrants. *The 7-Eleven in Southampton or (formerly) the Long Island Railroad Station in East Hampton.* See **labor tourist**.

hit the daily double *adj.* Born white and rich. *e.g., Paris Hilton.*

hit the trifecta *adj.* Born white, rich and male. *e.g., Luke Weil.* Also **won the Triple Crown**.

hitchhikers *n.* Cockroaches that ride CIDIOTS' luggage from Manhattan to the Hamptons.

holidaze *n.* The hangover after a long party weekend.

holy breadlock *n.* The condition of having married for money. *If you marry for money, you will surely earn it.*

HOMO *Acronym.* **Homeowner**.

homogenic *adj.* Neurotically hygienic. *"Leave your shoes outside and come in, but only step on the mat. Take a pair of paper slippers from the dispenser – make sure you don't step off the mat! Put the slippers on … Maria! Rufus pooped on the floor again, hurry and clean it up! Well, don't just stand there,* *come in! How are you?"* Conflation of **homeowner** and **hygienic.**

honesty *n.* A simple matter of economics.

honor *n.* Wealth.

hostage negotiator *n.* A homeowner or developer who holds a contractor captive with a promise of payment for services previously completed, but only after additional work has been performed.

house fluffing *v.* Installing temporary visual improvements such as art and furnishings to maximize the sale price of a house. **house fluffer** —*n.* Also **staging**.

house of cards *n.* **1.** A highly leveraged property, especially if purchased solely for status, that one is economically hard-pressed to maintain. **2.** A flimsy structure that will collapse with the first breath of wind. *A new, speculatively built* McMansion *in the Hamptons.*

humbrella *n.* A device such as a beach umbrella that is used to shield the view of sexual activity in a public place, such as at Peter's Pond Beach in Sagaponack. Also **humpbrella**.

humbrella

humility *n*. Resentful submission to one's superiors.

hummer *n*. **1**. A type of FUV. See **FUV**. **2**. A masculinity-boosting device.

hummerbird *n*. **1**. A flightless, invasive and highly destructive species, closely related to the dodo, that migrates to the Hamptons for the SILLY SEASON. **2**. A hand gesture commonly used to communicate with FUV drivers. See **FUV**.

Hummeroid *n*. **1**. An extremely irritating condition that consists of having a Hummer riding your ass while driving. **2**. The person driving the Hummer that is tailgating you.

hurricane bait *n*. **1**. Any oceanfront property. **2**. One who builds an oceanfront house in an area frequented by violent cyclonic storms.

hyperchondriac *n*. A person who is neurotically obsessed with their health. *A condition characterized by regular or repeated consultations with a variety of medical experts, often for third and fourth opinions, genetic sequencing for hereditary disease, head-to-toe MRI and CT scans, invasive exploratory procedures, etc., to confirm that one is indeed physically healthy, at least for the moment.*

hyperdating *n*. Dating many different people over a short period of time, preferably a different one each and every night. See **bed hopping**.

hyperparenting *n*. Obsessive micromanagement of a child's schedule and activities out of fear that one's child will underperform academically, socially or athletically. *A behavior that invariably guarantees that one's fears will be realized.* **hyperparent** —*v., n.* **hyperparental** —*adj.*

hyperpoliteness *n*. **1**. Disingenuous courtesy. See **curtesy**. **2**. Civility taken to the level of mockery. *e.g., Addressing a restaurant server or store clerk as "sir" or "madam".* **3**. A form of insincerity often used in combination with OBSESSIVE PERSISTENCE, usually in an attempt to attain something difficult to acquire, such as an item not on the restaurant's menu or a table at Bobby Van's on Saturday night.

idiocentric *adj.* **1.** At the center of one's own universe. **idiocentricity** —*n.* **2.** The belief that one is the center of the universe. [GREEK **idios** (one's own), LATIN **centrum** (center)]

ignoranus *n.* A person who is both ignorant and an asshole, a condition often compounded by the accumulation of money. See **False Authority Syndrome**.

I'm not really interested in money *Expression.* I'm only interested in money.

implant *n.* **1.** A car with a top speed in excess of three times the speed limit, usually found gridlocked in Hamptons summer traffic. **2.** A device used to treat erectile dysfunction.

incestuous amplification *n.* The reinforcement of a set of beliefs among like-minded people, leading to errors in judgment. *e.g., Buy-*

ing a Hummer, building a McMansion, *etc.* See **ridiculture**.

income stream *n.* A small CASHCADE.

inconspicuous consumption *n.* A mark of inferiority and cause for demerit.

inequity aversion *n.* The tendency to shun people of a different economic status than one's own. **inequity-averse** —*adj.*

inferior consumption *n.* Parvenu shopping. *Buying supermarket brand groceries, a* McMansion *in the Hamptons, hiring a* Feng Shui *decorator, etc.*

inferior decoration *n.* The art of bad taste. See **haut kitsch**.

In God We Trust *American Motto.* All others must pay cash.

inheritance powder *n.* Arsenic.

inside *adj.* **1.** Among a select group of people, such as the A-LIST. **2.** In prison.

instant forest *n.* Fully mature landscaping, especially trees of 24" or greater caliper, transplanted around a brand new house in a futile attempt to simulate an old-money environment. Antonym **cheapscape**.

instant forest

instant tan *n.* **1**. A tan in a bottle. **2**. The look of leisure time and travel to distant lands for only $10.95. *e.g., St. Tropez Auto Bronzant, Ambre Solaire Self-Tan, etc*. See **tanscaping**.

investment *n.* Any property in the Hamptons. See **vacation home**.

irrigation system *n.* **1**. A bar, nightclub or social hall. **2**. A liquor cabinet. **3**. A device for people who can't afford a gardener that automatically waters one's lawn, even when it is raining.

it's a deal *Expression*. A phrase indicating that a midpoint in bargaining has been reached and that tough negotiations are about to begin. See **cheese**.

it's only money *Expression.* A comment seemingly used to disparage the outlandish cost of one's POCKET ESTATE, FUV or other symbol of material excess while actually celebrating one's ability to make such stupendous and frivolous expenditures.

it wasn't expensive *Expression*. A phrase used, often with feigned embarrassment, in an attempt to convince others that one is not as wealthy as one appears to be.

Jaffe's First Law *Maxim.* "The value of a service is inversely proportional to its degree of completion." *The propensity of the wealthy to renegotiate the price of a service after it has been completed, or to avoid paying entirely.*

Jaffe's Second Law *Maxim.* "If you need a lawyer, it's already too late."

James Blonde *n.* A man who does something stupid while trying to act sophisticated. Also **uh-oh seven**. See **command performance**.

jet blonde *adj., n.* A woman with blonde hair and a black box.

jitnoid *n.* A HAMPTON JITNEY commuter.

John Dough *adj.* Just another dime a dozen multimillionaire.

joy-to-stuff ratio *n*. The amount of time spent enjoying life divided by the amount of time spent accumulating, maintaining and worrying about one's financial and material wealth.

junior mansion See **starter castle**.

junior millionaire *adj*. Having a net worth of at least ten million dollars. See **millionaire.**

junior mint *n*. An OVERLOADED young person. *A 20 year old with a Hamptons estate*. See **SPRICK**.

junk in the trunk *n*. **1**. Extra padding in the back, especially on an attractive woman. *"She's pretty, but she's got too much junk in the trunk."* **2**. Excess emotional or material baggage that one drags through life. *e.g., A string of ex-wives, a collection of vacation properties, etc.*

just a few changes *Expression*. A diminutive phrase used to describe the teardown and complete reconstruction of a STARTER CASTLE or MEGACOTTAGE or the construction of an addition that at the bare minimum doubles the size of the original structure. See **addition**.

justice *n*. The inability to buy one's way out of trouble. *The Aston Martin driver who picked up a bribery charge in addition to a speeding ticket.*

Ken doll *adj*. **1**. An athletic blonde, blue-eyed male with plastic values and zero personality. —*n*. **2**. Arm candy. **3**. A blank Chuck. See **blank chic**.

Kentucky bluegrass *n*. A pedigreed lawn.

Kodak moment *n*. Bumping elbows with a celebrity. See **touch of class**.

Kraft dinner *n*. The type of meal typically prepared in a show kitchen. See **show kitchen.**

labor tourist

label whore *n*. **1.** A person who wears name brand clothing and accessories, especially those of high cost, with the brand name or logo conspicuously displayed. *An unpaid walking advertisement for brand name merchandise.* **2.** A person who carries shopping bags from ritzy stores in a vain attempt to appear stylish or wealthy. Also **brand slut**. See **cost dropping**.

labialplasty *n*. Cosmetic surgery of the labia to improve appearance, often performed in conjunction with ANAL BLEACHING.

labor tourist *n*. A person who lives in one country but works in another. See **four footer**.

Lake Atlantic *Surfing. adj.* **1.** Flat; calm. —*n*. **2.** Summertime surf conditions on the East End. Antonym **surf's up**.

land yacht *n*. An extraordinarily large SUV.

landmine *n.* Hidden or camouflaged beach debris of the hazardous type; such as broken glass, dog poop, the still hot remains of a beach fire, etc.

landscraping *Literal* "earth removal." *n.* **1.** Of or relating to the destruction of wide swaths of the natural environment for replacement with man-made structures typically consisting of UP-SCALE MEGACOTTAGES with guest houses, tennis courts, swimming pools and acres of herbicide, pesticide and fungicide sprayed pedigree lawn, etc. **2.** The removal of all native species of vegetation in preparation for the transplantation of exotic imported foliage including fully mature trees. See **instant forest. landscrape** —*v.* [OLD ENGLISH **lond** (soil), OLD NORSE **skrapa** (erase)]

latte (lah·teh') *n.* A weak cappuccino made with extra milk specifically for the timid palates of Americans. *If ordered in Italy, one would receive a glass of plain milk.*

leisure sickness *n.* A rampant behavioral malady characterized by frenetic activity during one's time off from work, common among those who spend the majority of their time in the aggressive pursuit of money. See **relaxation**.

less than fabulous *adj.* Not on the A-LIST. *One who must wait in line at a restaurant, night club, etc.*

LIE *Oxymoronic Acronym.* **Long Island Expressway.** Also **Long Island Distressway.**

liedentity *n.* **1**. A false identity assumed to make restaurant reservations. See **reservation fraud**. **2**. A fictitious personal history intended to enhance one's status. *"I designed that house with Norman Jaffe."* See **foreploy**. **3**. A carefully constructed ego, especially if built from material goods. See **glass house**.

liposculpture *n.* Surgical transplant of fat cells from one place to another, undertaken with the desperate hope of making one appear somewhat more attractive, often with the opposite effect.

Lizzie Grubman Effect *n.* **1**. The inevitable result of growing up with the proverbial silver coke spoon; nannies and au pairs, world travel, access to celebrities, etc., everything one could possibly want or desire except for the love and attention of one's parents. **2**. Sociopathic behavior by the wealthy. *e.g., Going into a fit of rage and reversing, in Daddy's Mercedes FUV, over 16 people outside a nightclub at which one has been rejected.*

local *n.* **1**. A person who is under contract to purchase property in the Hamptons. **2**. A person who owns property in the Hamptons. **3**. A person who has lived in the Hamptons for more than five minutes. **4**. A person who lives in the Hamptons year-round. **5**. *Archaic.* A person born on the EAST END. *An East Ender*. **6**. A person whose great-grandparents were born on the EAST END. See **Bonacker**. **7**. A rude, uneducated person. **8**. A moron. *"I was stuck in traffic behind a local all the way from East Hampton."* See **staff**.

local price *n. Obsolete.* A discount for locals. *The practice of changing prices on a seasonal basis, rising for the SILLY SEASON and returning to normal after Labor Day. Since true locals are nearly extinct, and prices are no longer lowered when the season is over, local price has all but disappeared from common use.* See **local service**.

local service *n.* Preferred or otherwise expedited service for locals. *A practice that rewards those who provide the bread and butter of off-season business, often deliberately and pointedly performed in front of CIDIOTS and self-appointed MASTERS OF THE UNIVERSE.*

localization *v.* The process of transformation from CIDIOT to moron. See **local**.

Long Island Builder's Institute *Slang.* The Southampton Town Board.

Long Island Iced Tea *Recipe.* **1**. A drink consisting of vodka, gin, rum, tequila, and triple sec mixed with Coca Cola. **2**. A drink consisting of whatever alcohol is immediately available, either straight up or combined with whatever mixer is within reach.

Long Island lobster *n*. A lobster imported to Long Island from Maine.

lotto *n*. A retirement fund for people doing the Hamptons Shuffle. See **Hamptons Shuffle**.

lowball *n*. **1**. A medical condition common among the wealthy. —*v*. **2**. Make a purchase offer substantially below the asking price. See **mize**.

lowbread *adj*. Poor.

lucky sperm club See **hit the trifecta**.

Manhattan blonde *n.* Any one of thousands of indistinguishable blonde women fully bedecked in a tourist uniform consisting of tennis whites, jodhpurs and riding boots, etc., accessorized with diamond jewelry and Chanel or other brand name purse. See **jet blonde**.

manny (man'·ee) *n.* **1.** A male nanny. **2.** A mannequin seated in the driver's seat of a parked police car positioned so as to deter speeders.

manscaping *n.* The art of shaving and trimming one's body hair.

marginally rich *adj.* Barely able to afford to live in the Hamptons. See **destitute**.

marketecture *n.* **1.** The architecture of SPEC HOUSES. **2.** A style of architecture concerned solely with maximizing the sale value of specu-latively developed real estate. *A house with the maximum number of bedrooms with en-suite baths, a swimming pool,* SHOW KITCHEN, *security system, faux classical detailing, etc., applied in a manner to give the appearance of scale and opulence at the least pos-sible expense.* See **featuritis**.

mask of success *n.* The projection of an at-titude of boredom, as if one has already seen everything worth seeing too many times. *The simulation of a behavior assumed to belong to the up-per class.* See **happy look**.

mason's insurance *n. Construction Industry.* A panel of glass carefully set to block the flue of a newly constructed chimney. *The glass is dis-cretely broken out with a brick once full payment for the work has been received.*

masstige (mas·stej') *n.* **1.** The level of respect at which one is regarded by others for accumu-lation or display of mass-marketed consumer products such as Polo, BMW, Harley Davidson, Rolex, etc. **2.** The prestige of owning brand name consumer goods.

master of the universe *n.* **1**. The self-image of a person who has just purchased or rented a vacation house in the Hamptons. **2**. A person who is utterly incapable of doing their own laundry. See **MOTUS.**

maximalism *n.* A distinctly American school of thought that regards bigger as better. *If a 2,000 square foot house is good, a 20,000 square foot house must be better.* See **big**.

McMansion *n.* **1**. Tasteless architectural fast food. **2**. A super-sized house. **3**. An oversize house speculatively built with the cheapest materials and labor for quick sale to uneducated social climbers desperate to improve their status. *A massive pseudo- or neoclassical style house built on a too-small lot and readily identified by an eyebrow roof window, fiberglass porch columns, acres of soon to be peeling paint and a Range Rover in the driveway.* **4**. A philistine's status symbol. **5**. A house painter's dream. See **annuity**.

McMansion farm *n.* A subdivision of too-big houses crammed together on too-small lots.

McMoron *n*. A freshly minted multi-million-aire who rushes to the Hamptons to buy a MCMANSION.

MDL *Acronym*. **Mutton Dressed as Lamb.** *Expression*. A mature woman, often in her 50's or older, who dresses as if she were in her 20's. See **fifty-footer**.

megacottage *n*. **1**. An absurdly large weekend house; a MCMANSION. **2**. A self-defeating "getaway" house that requires substantial expense for operation and maintenance. See **pig-out.**

meme (mee'·mee) *n*. One who is excessively preoccupied with oneself. *"I don't care if it's Sunday. I don't care if it's your daughter's communion. I don't care about you at all. All I care about is me, me, me! Now get over here and clean my swimming pool right now!"* See **screaming meme**.

Midas effect *n*. The unique and seemingly effortless ability of wealth to turn anything into shit.

Midas touch *n*. **1**. The tendency of money to multiply itself despite the gross errors of those who have it. *e.g., Buy a badly designed, poorly built house on a noisy road at the top of the market and sell it in a year for double the purchase price.*

MDL

million dollar smile *n.* The expression on a real estate broker's face at a Hamptons closing.

millionaire *adj.* **1.** A poor person. **2.** One who cannot afford a second (or first) home in the Hamptons. *Finance.* **3.** A person with an annual income of at least one million dollars. See **junior millionaire**. **4.** *Obsolete.* A person with a net worth of at least one million dollars.

missed the gravy boat *Expression.* **1.** Failed to exercise an opportunity to purchase real estate in the Hamptons before the latest boom in prices. **2.** The feeling that the vacation house one has just bought could have, until very recently, been purchased for a substantially lower price.

mize (my·ze) *v.* **1.** Attempt to negotiate the purchase of a clearly priced item or service. **2.** Attempt to avoid sales tax by offering to pay cash. **mizer** —*n.*

mizernaire (my·zer'·nair) *n.* **1.** A person who lives in a rent controlled apartment in Manhattan and owns a vacation house in the Hamptons. **2.** A wealthy person who aggressively negotiates the price of every purchase, no matter how small. Also **blue chipper**.

mizery (my·zer'·ee) *n*. The condition or state of being unable to negotiate a discount.

mobile (mo'·bile) *n*. Foul language screamed into a cell phone. *e.g., The* CIDIOT *screaming obscenities into his cell phone while pushing his child in a stroller down Job's Lane in Southampton.* **going mobile** —*v*. See **degradation ceremony**.

mobile home *n*. An automobile filled with a homeless person's belongings. Also **mobile office**.

modelist *n*. A attractive woman, often an aging former model, who uses her appearance to acquire benefits from men such as use of a Hamptons summerhouse, restaurant invitations, sports or theater tickets, etc., without the sex that is often customary in such an exchange. See **AMT**.

modelizer *n*. One who pursues models lecherously. **modelize** —*v*.

modernism *n*. A formerly avant-garde style of architecture now considered déclassé by those pretending to be old money. *The reason there are so many* NEOCLASSICAL MCMANSIONS *in the Hamptons.*

modest See **aw shucks**.

mom job *n.* Surgical procedures used to restore the appearance of a woman's body after child birth. *e.g., Breast lift, tummy tuck, etc.* Also **mommy makeover**.

mommiac *n.* A maniacal mother, invariably accompanied by child, often in a stroller, who emotionally detonates when impeded. *e.g., The woman who, while trespassing with offspring and nanny at Foster Farm, exploded when politely asked to introduce herself.* Conflation of **mommy** and **maniac**. See **emotional detonation**.

moneyed *adj.* Noble.

monirexia *n.* A psychological disorder characterized by an abnormal fear of becoming poor, a distorted self-image and persistent compulsion to acquire money, often accompanied by obsessive negotiation of purchases, frivolous lawsuits, etc.

monster house *n.* **1.** A house that is too big for its lot. **2.** An oversized house, especially one that doesn't match the scale or style of neighboring architecture. Also **Frankenhouse.**

Montauk *n.* A place that is so far out it's beyond the Hamptons. Also **The End**.

moron *n.* A carpenter who cut a board too short. *"But it's only short on one end!"* Conflation of **more** and **on**. See **staff**.

moronodon *n.* **1.** A person whose volume of consumption pushes not just their own species but all life on planet Earth towards extinction. See **exemptionalist**. **2.** A person of such colossal stupidity that they are on the verge of self-extinction, a behavior often demonstrated while driving in the Hamptons. See **MVA**.

MOTUS (moe'·tuss) *Acronym.* **Master of the Universe Syndrome**. The belief that one is ranked a step above POTUS (President of the United States). See **egotheism**.

muffin top *n.* The roll of flesh that hangs over the waistline of one's pants, especially if one is wearing a midriff-baring top. See **spandex rule**.

MVA *Acronym.* **Motor Vehicle Accident.** *The inevitable result of too many* TIMED-OUT MASTERS OF THE UNIVERSE *competing against each other in the Hamptons.*

name dropper *n.* One who casually or pointedly mentions the names of celebrities or the very wealthy in a calculated manner, often using first names or nicknames specifically to imply personal familiarity with them. *While name dropping is done with the intention of increasing one's social status, it often has the opposite effect.* **name dropping** —*v.*

nanny *n.* A surrogate mother. See **au pair.**

nanny & me *n.* An educational or recreational class for toddlers and their nannies. *Formerly* **mommy & me**.

nanny-cam *n.* A video camera, often small enough to be concealed inside a child's toy, attached to a recording device and used to spy on nannies or other household staff.

nanny envy *n*. **1**. Emotions of jealously towards a nanny, especially one that receives more affection from your child than you do. **2**. Emotions of jealousy and feelings of resentment towards a nanny justified by the amount of time the nanny spends with one's children. **3**. Feelings of jealousy towards women whose children have nannies.

nanny withdrawal *n*. An emotional condition, similar to the grief felt when a loved one dies, experienced by children when their nanny quits or is fired, often on a seasonal or annual basis.

neoclassical *adj., n*. **1**. An architectural style based on recreating the appearance of classical architecture, most often with a highly restrictive budget that defeats the very purpose of the project. **2**. The preferred style of the NOUVEAU RICHE as it provides a high degree of social conformity, eliminating the risks of individuality. **3**. The standard style for all McMANSIONS. Also **pseudoclassical**.

Neptune cocktail *n*. *Surfing.* Seawater ingested during a wipeout. See **sand facial**.

neurodiversity *n.* The seemingly endless variety of neurotic behaviors and neurological disorders displayed by the wealthy. *The woman at a restaurant who asks for boiling water so she can wash the silverware at the table.* **neurodiverse** —*adj.*

never count someone else's money *Adage.* "Don't judge a book by its cover."

new money *n.* **1**. A type of money reputedly not as good as old money, but one that is certainly better than no money at all. **2**. A lifestyle based on the display of wealth and knowledge of the best things to consume, aimed not at one's would-be peers but at all those below them. See **parvenu**. **3**. A lifestyle in which one must constantly be on guard for changing tastes and styles so as not to appear ignorant, or even worse, poor. —*ad*j. **4**. Crass; pretentious. *A Mc-* MANSION *with an* INSTANT FOREST.

New York Magazine *n.* The official weekly cultural guide for SHEEPLE.

New York Times, the *n.* The official daily cultural guide for SHEEPLE.

Nick and Toni's See **Slick and Phony's.**

night of the living dead *n.* **1.** A formal affair, especially one attended by A-LIST and TABLOID PEOPLE. **2.** A party at a SHARE HOUSE, especially at the end of the SILLY SEASON.

noblesse oblige (no·bless′ oh·bleej′) *French. n.* The obligation of those of inferior rank to cater to the whims and fantasies of the wealthy.

NoHi *abbr.* See **north of the highway**.

noisy jewelry *n.* **1.** Jewelry that you can hear coming. Also **bling** or **bling bling**. **2.** Jewelry or other decoration that is blinding in its reflectivity. **3.** Ostentatious personal ornamentation. *e.g., A custom* CHEVY SUBDIVISION *with 3,000 watt subwoofer stereo and highly polished oversize chrome wheels with spinners.*

north of the highway *n* **1.** The geographic area north of the Montauk Highway, away from the Atlantic Ocean. **2.** The relative value of real estate or the wealth of people with houses there. —*adj.* **3.** Cheap; low class. *"They have a house north of the highway."* Also **NoHi**. See **south of the highway.**

not enough See **too much**.

night of the living dead

nouveau* poor** (nu´·vo poor´) *adj.* Newly poor people, especially those without the occupational skills necessary to make a living or the social skills necessary to navigate working class society. Antonym ***nouveau riche.

obscenely rich *adj.* More than filthy rich. A self-deprecating expression often used by the über rich, seemingly to disparage their wealth but actually to celebrate it. *"I'm not über rich, I'm just obscenely rich."* See **über rich.**

obsessive persistence *n.* A behavior common to spoiled children and the very wealthy.

obtainium *n.* **1.** Dumpster pickings. See **Caldor East**. **2.** Yard sale leftovers. **3.** Discarded or forgotten objects found by chance. **4.** Something that can be or has been stolen. Antonym **unobtainium**.

oceanfront *adj., n.* Real property located on an ocean beach that is subject to massive crowds of people, steady erosion, and is at substantial risk of being wiped clean in a hurricane. *The most expensive type of property in the Hamptons.* See **hurricane bait**.

oceanview *adj., n.* A marketing term used to describe property from which the ocean is visible, often through a narrow view-shaft, raising the sale price considerably. See **viewshaft**.

off-season *adj., n. Obsolete.* A time of year when the number of LOCALS in the Hamptons exceeds the number of CIDIOTS.

old money *n.* **1.** A type of money reputedly better than any other. **2.** Wealth inherited from generations long dead. **3.** A class style based on quality of behavior, often eccentric and incestuous, rather than the display of wealth, which is ridiculed by NEW MONEY for its ignorance yet aspired to for its simplicity. *e.g., A* BIG DOG *driving a rusty '79 Buick station wagon.* —*ad*j. **4.** Royal.

ostrichcized (ost·rich'·sizd) *adj.* Shunned solely because of one's wealth or lack thereof. **ostrichcize** —*v.*

other Hampton, the *n.* Any low-income neighborhood in the Hamptons. *e.g., Hillcrest Terrace in Southampton, Morris Park in East Hampton.*

out-castled *v.* The diminution of one's Mc-MANSION, POCKET ESTATE or STARTER CASTLE by the construction of an even larger one next door. Also **out-templed.**

overloaded *adj.* **1**. Overly rich. **2**. Too rich or wealthy; having more money than one knows what to do with. *e.g., Playing at real estate development on multiple properties in* SOUTHAMPTON VILLAGE *simply because one has nothing better to do.* Also **stuffed**.

overstatement *n.* **1**. A McMANSION or MEGA-COTTAGE in the Hamptons. **2**. A thick wad of singles carefully wrapped with a one hundred dollar bill. *A Jewish bankroll.* **3**. Any display of wealth.

pacemaker

pacemaker *n*. A CIDIOT in a hurry.

package *n*. One's body or physical attributes.

packaging *n*. One's clothes or outfit.

padding *n*. The amount added to invoices by contractors in anticipation of not getting a final payment. [LOW GERMAN **pad** (bundle of straw to lie on)]

pandephonium *n*. The sudden panic and confusion experienced by all cell phone users in the area when a cell phone rings. Also **ringxiety**.

panzerwagen (pant·sur·vag'·en) *German, literal* "armored wagon." *n*. A Mercedes G500 or G55, especially if carrying a full platoon of shock troops on an assault mission to a retail or culinary objective such as The Gap or the Candy Kitchen. See **FUV**.

pap (pop) *v.* **1**. To stalk for photographs or a news story. **papped** —*adj.* (pop·t) **2**. Ambushed by photographers or journalists. *Derivation*: *paparazzi*.

paper the file *v.* **1**. Create a massively thick legal file solely to justify an exorbitant attorney's fee. *e.g., A 600 page stack of documents at a real estate closing, 95% of which are utterly useless except as a means of justifying a high five-figure fee for handling the closing on a multi-million dollar property.* Also **billing by the pound**. **2**. Generate exhaustive documentation of an architectural or construction project in preparation for the legal action that will invariably be necessary to collect payment for services rendered or to defend against a lawsuit initiated to avoid payment due for work that has been successfully completed. See **Jaffe's First Law.**

parking lot effect *n.* Landscape or garden lighting surrounding a McMANSION or MEGA-COTTAGE that is bright and evenly distributed, much like the lighting in a typical shopping center parking lot.

party whore See **social slut**.

parvenu (par·ve·noo') *French. adj.* A person who has recently or suddenly acquired wealth, importance, position, or the like, but has not yet developed the manners, dress, education, surroundings, etc. appropriate to their position. Synonym **nouveau riche.**

patience *n.* The withholding of arrogance for a brief period of time.

penniless *adj.* No longer a multi-millionaire. See **destitute**.

peripherals *pl.n.* **1**. A person's entourage. *e.g., Bodyguards.* Also **perfs**. *Singular* **peripheral 2**. A person's date, especially if primarily for image. Also **perf**. See **blank chic.**

permanent place setting *n.* A table in a restaurant that has been purchased by an individual for their exclusive use. *"No, sir, I'm sorry. That table is reserved."*

personal manager *n.* A person hired to perform the basic functions that another is incapable of such as laundry, shopping, answering the telephone, walking the dog, etc. Also **banana peeler.** See **acquired incompetence**.

pest control device *n.* **1**. Landscaping, fencing, etc. intended to screen the view of neighboring property. See **spite hedge**. **2**. A fence installed to prevent access to the public beach in front of a private oceanfront property. **3**. A security gate, call box, driveway sensor or other device preventing, controlling or monitoring access to property. **4**. A caretaker or estate manager.

pettygree *n.* A less than desirable family tree.

philandrapist (fi·land·ra′·pist) *n.* A real estate developer, especially one that acts as if anything they build is an improvement over what already exists, including nature. *"J.R., meet Carol. She's a philandrapist, too."*

pig-out *n., v.* **1**. A grotesque display of wealth. *e.g., A birthday party for a five-year-old with three hundred guests held at an oceanfront estate in Southampton, catered by Balducci's and featuring acrobats, jugglers, clowns, mimes, caricature artists, live music by Christina Aguilera, amusement park rides, fireworks, etc. —n.* **2**. Voracious consumption of material goods. *e.g., Building a* MEGACOTTAGE, *collecting vacation properties, etc.* **pigging out**, **pigged out**.

pillow talk *Expression. Construction Industry.* Sweet talk a subcontractor. *Promises made to tradesmen such as tickets to Knicks games, work on other projects, bonuses, etc., in an effort to secure favors such as discounts, immediate service, etc.*

place setting *n.* The art of selecting a seat at a restaurant for the highest possible status.

playstation *n.* A vacation house in the Hamptons.

plush toy *n.* **1.** A wealthy person that one keeps around, usually by means of sex, for financial support. **2.** A meal ticket. See **ATM.**

pocket estate *adj.* **1.** A poor man's estate. —*n.* **2.** A marketing term used to sell houses to people who can't afford a proper estate. See **estate**.

poisonal check *n.* A check that is destined to bounce.

poisonal space *n.* A vacation house that was so expensive or otherwise frustrating that one can never be happy or comfortable in it. *e.g., A poorly built house that requires constant* *maintenance; a custom house that ran way over budget and took several years to complete, the house where one's spouse was caught having an affair, etc.*

Polo Effect *n.* Social and economic effects on a community directly attributable to national and international franchises and high-end retailers. *Loss of community character, rising prices, reduction in wages, etc. due to a surplus of chain stores and franchises such as Gucci, Ralph Lauren, Saks Fifth Avenue, Starbucks, etc.* See **golden ghetto**.

pondfront *adj., n.* Real property located on a pond, often plagued by mosquitoes, no-see-ums (biting midges), flooded basements, etc. *The third highest valued property type on the EAST END.*

Poop Patrol *n.* An indispensable luxury service that collects dog droppings from one's yard on a regular schedule. *"We're On Duty For You."*

poor man's beach *n.* **1.** *Obsolete.* The beach at the end of Ocean Road in Bridgehampton. **2.** Any beach that does not require a parking fee or permit.

poor rich *adj., n.* **1.** Wealthy people who complain they never have any money. See **crying**

poor. **2**. Wealthy people who agonize over or complain about the cost of every purchase, no matter how small. *"I was going to buy a nice card to go with the teacher's gift, but it was $4 and that seemed so expensive."* **3**. Wealthy people who can't afford a second (or third or fourth) house in the Hamptons. **4**. Working class people whose property has quadrupled (or more) in value but are barely able to afford to live in the Hamptons.

poorist *n*. A person who vacations close to home to save money. See **day tripper**.

porcupine *n*. **1**. A Porsche. *"What's the difference between a Porsche and a porcupine? A porcupine has the pricks on the outside."* **2**. Any expensive sports car. See **implant**.

poser *adj*. **1**. One who adopts the behaviors and attributes of different social class than the one to which they belong. *e.g., Pretending to be a local*. —*n*. **2**. *Surfing*. A surfer wannabe, readily identified by a Hawaiian shirt, Huarache sandals and a surf board that is never removed from the roof rack of a late model Range Rover. Also **Benny**. See **Chubby Checker**. [French **poseur** (affect an attitude)]

post modernism *n.* **1.** A mixture of contemporary and neoclassical architecture styles that is admired by CIDIOTS, who believe it projects high culture and refined taste. **2.** An architectural style that can best be described as minimalist NEOCLASSICAL with FEATURITIS.

Potato Prince *n.* The son of an East End farmer who will one day inherit a family farm worth more than the GNP of a small European country. *Projecting an aura of humility, Potato Princes are often found driving tractors or maintaining farm equipment.* Also **spud stud** *or* **spud royalty.** *Feminine* POTATO PRINCESS. See **Sagaponack**.

Potato Princess *n.* The daughter of an East End farmer who will one day inherit a family farm with a value equivalent to a modest oil sheikdom. *Projecting an aura of humility, Potato Princesses are often found working in the farm fields or running the family's roadside farm stand.* Also **spud royalty.** *Masculine* POTATO PRINCE. See **Sagaponack**.

Potato Royalty *n.* The near divine status of down-to-earth local farmers whose land value has made them CENTIMILLIONAIRES. Also **spud royalty.**

poverty See **crying poor**.

potato prince

power See **black helicopter moment**.

power bitch *n.* An arrogant faux Buddhist, often seen at power yoga classes wearing Thai fisherman's pants with diamond jewelry and a smugly superior attitude.

price up *v.* **1.** *Construction Industry.* Create forged subcontractor invoices to justify fraudulent construction charges and fees. *"John, price up a new roof for the South Main Street job."* **2.** *Retail Trade.* Raise prices in anticipation of the SILLY SEASON.

pride *n.* Taking more than one needs. See **entitlement**.

private club *n.* A weekend house used for weekday parties by service staff. *e.g., The Southampton house where a raucous party was thrown every Wednesday night by house watchers, pool cleaners, landscapers, window washers, etc., with full knowledge that the cleaning service, scheduled for Thursday, would provide thorough clean up and complete restocking at the owner's expense.* Also **after hours club**.

private reserve *n.* A formerly scenic area of land, the development rights for which have been acquired for the public benefit, that has been intentionally hidden behind a MᴄMᴀɴꜱɪᴏɴ ꜰᴀʀᴍ or dense screen of landscaping to increase the value and privacy of adjacent property. Also **agricultural reserve**.

privet compound *n*. An enclosed, highly secure area designed to protect MASTERS OF THE UNIVERSE and their offspring from exposure to nature or humanity in any of their virulent forms. See **big house**.

privet sector *n*. The estate section, where privacy is assured by immaculately pruned towering privet hedges, often 16 feet or more in height.

privilege *n*. An exclusive license, granted by wealth and wholly without responsibility, to be completely and exclusively preoccupied with oneself. See **MOTUS**.

pro-detail *Euphemism*. Anal.

proletarian drift *n*. **1**. The tendency for elements of high culture to appeal to the lower socio-economic classes. **2**. The tendency for originally upscale products and services to become popular with the working class. **3**. The reduction in price and quality necessary to provide what were once luxury goods and services to the middle and lower classes. [LATIN **proletarius** (citizen of the lowest class), MIDDLE DUTCH **drift** (to drive)] Also **prole drift**.

prosperity blight *n.* The negative effects of wealth on areas such as the Hamptons, where a child's one-hour tennis lesson costs $100 and summer day camp costs $1,200 a week. See **golden ghetto**.

pump and dump *n., v.* Quick, inexpensive visual improvements to an aging or decaying property to improve its resale value. Also **pump the dump**. See **house fluffing**.

punch list *n.* **1.** A list of often niggling complaints and demands for work on a construction project that must be completed before negotiation over final payment can begin. **2.** A device used to justify non-payment of a contractor's invoice. **3.** A list that makes the one responsible for the items on it feel like punching the one who made it.

Que Mart (kay mahrt) *n*. A Latino marketplace in Bridgehampton. See **labor tourist**.

queen of clubs *n*. **1**. A party girl. **2**. An overbearing spouse or girlfriend.

queen of diamonds *n*. **1**. A woman who judges men by the size of their summer houses in the Hamptons. **2**. A woman who dates or marries a man specifically for his money and prestige. Variation of **gold-digger.** See **plush toy.**

queue rage (kyu raj) *n*. **1**. Anger over having to wait in line. *What the MASTER OF THE UNIVERSE displayed when forced to wait behind his inferiors.* See **timed-out**. **2**. Anger over being rejected from the express lane because one has too many items. See **do you know who I am? 3**. Anger at being in an express checkout line behind someone with too many items, or against a person who has cut in front of one while in a line.

ransom factor *n*. **1**. The tendency of people of wealth to use the high cost of legal action as justification to break contracts and refuse to pay for services rendered. *"I can pay my lawyer more than you make."* See **Jaffe's First Law**. **2**. The inability to contest one who has broken a contract or refused to pay for services provided due to the high cost of legal fees. See **Jaffe's Second Law**.

real faux *Oxymoron. adj.* Genuinely phony.

recreation sight *n*. **1**. Attractive, scantily clad girls. *e.g. Surfer girls at Ditch Plains.* **2**. A nude beach. *e.g. Peter's Pond beach in Sagaponack.*

recreational facility *n*. A place or area devoted to community athletic events or sporting activities. *e.g., The Atlantic Golf Club (membership fee: $575,000) or the Sebonack Golf Club (membership fee: $650,000, annual dues: $12,000).*

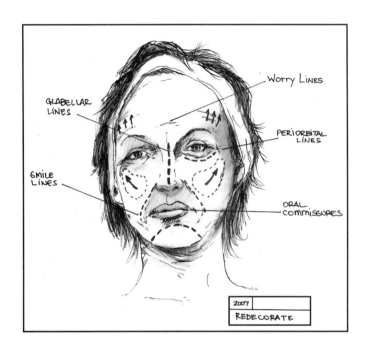

redecorate

recycle *v.* **1**. *Real Estate*. Speculatively convert a distressed property into lucrative real estate. See **pump and dump**. **2**. *Construction Industry*. Steal building materials from one project for use on another, for which both owners are charged accordingly. **3**. Hold a yard sale.

red carpet dermatology *n*. Nonsurgical procedures such as Botox injections to relax muscle tone, Restylane injections to fill wrinkles, microdermabrasion, etc., carried out in preparation for an upcoming social event.

redecorate *v*. Attempt to maintain or increase one's social status by changing appearance rather than substance. *e.g., Undergo plastic surgery.*

relative deprivation *n*. The insecurity of the rich in regard to their wealth and status in society.

relaxation *n*. Vigorous, competitive activity unrelated to work. **relax** —*v. e.g., Power yoga, obsessive competitiveness at golf, tennis, etc.*

renovation *n*. **1**. A construction project in which a house, especially one that is new or in perfect condition due to recent renovations, is completely rebuilt. **2**. A construction project in which an entire house is demolished and replaced one component at a time rather than completely razed and rebuilt. See **teardown. 3**. Plastic surgery or its results.

rent-a-friend *n*. **1**. Someone who is happy to come along, but only if you are paying. See **modelist. 2**. A professional escort.

renterror (ren·ter'·ror) *n*. **1**. A summer tenant from Hell. *"Hello? This is your tenant calling to advise you that the air conditioning is broken. I'll have you know that we are very rich and are used to far better treatment than this. If you don't have the air conditioning repaired by six p.m. we will be staying, at your expense, at the Maidstone Arms until we can move back into the house."* **2**. A summer vacation rental from Hell. *A rented summer house that is untenable due to noise, smell, failure of mechanical systems, infestations of rats, fleas, cockroaches, etc.*

rescue call *n*. A call made to a cell phone at a prearranged time specifically to provide the recipient with an excuse to leave a social engagement. *"Give me a rescue call at 8:15."* Also **SOS**.

reservation fraud *n*. A reservation falsely made in the name of a celebrity for the purpose of getting a table at a fully booked restaurant or nightspot. See **liedentity**.

reservation redundancy *n.* Multiple reservations made in various restaurants for the same date and time so as to keep one's entertainment options open, often made under assumed names to avoid black booking. See **black book.**

rich *adj.* Highly ironic. *e.g., The multimillionaire who can't get a plumber to fix the backed up toilet in his Hamptons vacation house.* See **suck down.**

rich as Croesus (kree·shus) *Expression.* Having legendary wealth. *Croesus was an ancient king who established the first gold refinery and introduced the use of minted coinage.* Also **über rich.**

rich kid killer *n.* An expensive imported high performance motorcycle. *e.g., A 198 mph 205 hp $65,000 Ducati Desmosedici RR.*

rich man's Levittown *n.* Any subdivision in the Hamptons. See **prosperity blight.**

richter scale (rich'·ter skal) *n.* A comparative gauge of success, as measured by one's wealth, on which garden variety millionaires don't even register. See **big dog.**

ridiculture (rid'·i·kul'·chur) *n.* Popular culture based on dubious precedents. *e.g., Wearing one's* *pants well below the hips, driving a Hummer, build-ing a* MEGACOTTAGE *in the Hamptons, etc.* Confla-tion of **ridiculous** and **culture**.

roach coach *n*. **1**. A Hampton Jitney. See **Them**. **2**. A moving van packed with a CIDIOT'S furnishings, inside which cockroaches travel to the Hamptons. See **hitchhikers**. **3**. A food service vehicle that caters to businesses and construction sites.

Rolex rider *n*. **1**. One who is equipped with an expensive brand new or perfectly restored clas-sic motorcycle and is unable or unwilling to ride it. *e.g., A motorcyclist with a tailored leather riding outfit, custom Shoei helmet with built-in voice-ac-tivated cell phone and intercom, a Breguet, Patek Philippe, Rolex or other name brand luxury wrist-watch and a brand new or extremely low-mileage top-of-the-line custom Harley Davidson or special order Orange County Chopper that is usually found parked in a garage or, upon rare occasions, in front of a trendy restaurant, but only during daylight hours.* **2**. A make-believe motorcyclist who is shunned by any real biker for whom a motorcycling is a lifestyle rather than an accessory.

rubberneck *n*. A window-shopping tourist who can't afford to purchase anything more expensive than an ice cream cone, often seen browsing, but never buying, in front of expensive stores on Newtown Lane in East Hampton or Job's Lane in Southampton. See **poorist**.

S

sacred *adj.* Expensive. See **spirituality**.

sacrificial lamb *n.* **1**. A child maintained only for the sake of appearances. *A necessary ornament.* **2**. A child, often adopted, to impress others and enhance the status of the parent or parents. *A trophy child.* **3**. The neglected child of a wealthy person or couple. *e.g., A child whose parents provide everything except love and attention.* See **Lizzie Grubman Effect.**

sacrilegious *adj.* Out of fashion. See **divine**.

Sagaponack *n.* A place where farmers are CENTIMILLIONAIRES and the only retail establishment features lobster salad at $100 per pound.

Salvation Armani *n.* Quality fashion found at yard sales and thrift shops.

sand facial *n.* *Surfing.* Dermal abrasion from wiping out and being dragged face first along the ocean floor. See **Neptune cocktail**.

sand trap *n*. Sinking millions of dollars into an oceanfront house that could easily be washed away in the next Nor'easter.

sandbag *n*. A less-than-attractive woman sunbathing. Also **sandhag**.

sandcastle *n*. An oceanfront estate.

sandhog *n*. The owner of an oceanfront house who treats the public beach in front of it as if it were private property. *e.g., The actor who fenced off the public beach in front of his Sagaponack house.*

sanitrashion (san·i·tray'·shen) *Literal* "sanitize trash." *n*. The act of removing all traces of personal information and identity from one's household garbage prior to dumping it in a restaurant or construction site dumpster, public refuse container, on a nature trail, etc., in order to assure security and prevent possible legal repercussions. See **trashole**.

sausage fest *n*. **1**. A gay beach, such as Two Mile Hollow in East Hampton or Fowler's in Southampton, especially one where Speedos are routinely packed with kielbasa or other faux meat. **2**. Any bar, nightclub, party or other event that is attended exclusively or primarily by males.

sausage fest

scene whore *n.* A person who attends every possible social event, including funerals, at which celebrities or other notables may be present. Scene whores are easily recognized as they are always overdressed and never have anyone to converse with except for other scene whores, who avoid each other like the plague out of fear of being compromised. *The East Hampton art gallery owner who went to the funeral of a renowned architect wearing a veil, as if she were his wife.*

schneider *v.* **1.** Eliminate one's competition by buying them out. **2.** Choke to death on one's own fabulous success. *Origin: Allan Schneider, the undisputed king of Hamptons real estate, who choked to death on not one, but two pieces of steak after a day spent drinking in celebration of the purchase of a real estate office in Amagansett that further expanded his empire.* **schneidered** *—adj.*

screaming meme *n.* A particularly loud or shrill meme. See **meme**.

screwercide *n.* A self-imposed CASHTASTRO-PHE. *e.g., An extra-marital affair that results in the loss of one's meal ticket.*

SCUM *Acronym.* **Self Centered Urban Male**.

service charge *n.* A behavioral tax added to the bill of a belligerent, impatient or overly demanding customer. Also **aggrichvation fee**. See **aggrichvation**.

shadow yacht *n.* **1**. A service and supply ship with quarters for security personnel and additional staff, storage facilities, helipad, automobiles, motor launches, jet skis, submarine, etc. that accompanies one's yacht. **2**. A component of a personal seagoing fleet.

shags to riches *Expression.* Sleeping one's way to the top. See **queen of diamonds**.

shake and bake *n.* **1**. A previously created architectural design resold to clients deemed unworthy of an original design effort. **2**. A rehashed architectural design with minimal modifications. *A custom spec house.* **3**. The architecture of McMansions.

share house *n.* A house illegally rented to a large number of people on a time sharing basis, such as alternate weekends *"I'm only paying $3,500 for my share in Water Mill."* Also **hampster cage**.

sheeple *pl. n.* Easily led people following each other, herded by insecurity, peer pressure, popular culture, mass-marketing and other dogs of conformity. *e.g., The people who suddenly and without warning descended in droves upon Breadzilla in Wainscott, but only for black and white cookies, and only after they were mentioned in* THE NEW YORK TIMES, *an approved* CULTURAL GUIDE.

shitterati *n.* **1.** Poorly behaved celebrities featured in the media. *e.g., Paris Hilton, Sean Combs, etc.* See **tabloid people**. **2.** Highly unfashionable celebrities. **3.** Attendees at many Hamptons events and soirees, such as the HAMPTON CLASSIC.

show kitchen *n.* A food preparation center outfitted with the latest commercial grade appliances including multiple sinks, refrigerators, dishwashers and appliance garages; exotic imported granite countertops; All-Clad cookware; William Henry custom cutlery, etc., especially if never used except to microwave defrost or reheat pre-prepared food. See **cold war**.

sidewalk sale *n.* The less than fabulous people hanging around a nightclub at closing time hoping to find someone with whom to conclude their evening. See **less than fabulous.**

silly season *n.* The period of time between Memorial Day and Labor Day, when the population of CIDIOTS in the Hamptons quintuples.

single digit millionaire *adj.* Having a net worth of less than ten million dollars. Also **junior millionaire**. See **affluent**.

SKI *Acronym.* **Spend the kid's inheritance**.

slaughterhouse *n.* A singles bar where the patrons are desperate.

Slick and Phony's *Slang.* Nick and Toni's Restaurant in East Hampton Village, a celebrity and wannabe hangout.

slimber (sly·mer) *n.* **1.** A person who thinks a reservation at NICK AND TONI'S will improve their social status. **2.** A NAME DROPPER. **3.** A COST DROPPER. **slimbey** —*adj.* **4.** Shallow; phony; affected. Conflation of **social** and **climber**.

sloppy tits *n.* Natural, un-enhanced female breasts. See **boob job**.

slumming *v.* Hanging out in a squalid area. *"We spent two weeks slumming in Southampton."* See **Eurotrash**.

small world effect *n.* The high likelihood of the wealthy to run into each other because of their tendency to frequent the same places. *e.g., NICK AND TONI'S in East Hampton, the Little Nell in Aspen, Hotel Mirabeau in Zermatt, etc.*

smart house *n.* A house equipped with a wide variety of technological features (including digitally controlled programmable climate, lighting, entertainment, maintenance, food preparation systems, etc., all made by different manufacturers and supplied with lengthy, extensively detailed and often incomprehensible operating manuals) that is exceedingly difficult to operate, even more so when it is only used occasionally, such as for weekend getaways. *The reason the digital clock on the $9,400 TMIO refrigerated internet-controlled double wall oven is always blinking "12:00".* See **cold war**.

smell test *n.* **1.** The practice of using whatever means are necessary to sniff out the business and legal history of a potential client. *e.g., Hire a private investigator to perform a thorough background check on the owner of a project one is considering bidding on.* **2.** An intuitive sense developed after years of experience dealing with BLUE CHIPPERS. *"I was thinking of sending him a proposal, but he didn't pass the smell test."*

snob appeal *Oxymoron*. Appeal is one of a number of things that snobs lack.

snob effect *n*. **1**. The desire to purchase something only because it is expensive. *e.g., A house in the Hamptons, a diamond encrusted computer mouse, etc.* **2**. The tendency for the price of a product or service to increase when it is perceived to improve one's social status.

social climber *n*. One who attempts to scale a mountain of insecurity by purchasing the most expensive climbing gear available.

social demotion *n*. Reduction of one's social class due to a faux pas or uncontrollable behavior. *e.g., A seemingly upper class person who is immediately reclassified when they try to wheedle a discount.*

social dominance *n*. The act of throwing one's weight around, demonstrated by the ability to get a table at Nick and Toni's just by showing up. See **black card**.

social insecurity *n*. Fear or unease about one's position in society. *"My assistant has a nicer summer house than I do – I'm going to have to fire him."* See **status quotient.**

social promotion *n*. An increase in rank based solely on money. *The inclusion of swimming pool contractor John Tortorella alongside Martha Stewart, Billy Joel, Leonardo DiCaprio, Ron Perelman, Steven Spielberg, etc. in* HAMPTONS MAGAZINE'S *listing of notable people.*

social recession *n*. Loss of status, most often due to CASHTRATION. *e.g., Losing one's ability to get a table at* NICK AND TONI'S *just by showing up.*

social script *n*. The role one performs for a particular audience, such as those who have employed one to work on their Hamptons summer house. See **beggar's waltz**.

social security *n*. Owning a house in the Hamptons.

social Siberia *adj*. The Hamptons in the off-season. *Locally known as Heaven.*

social slut *n*. **1**. One who attends every possible social event, even if only for a few minutes squeezed in between other events. **2**. A person who not only never refuses an invitation, but one who lives to seek them out. Also **party whore**.

sodomist *n.* A person who is obsessed with the quality of their lawn at the expense of all other life on the planet.

SoHa (so·hah') *abbr.* Verbal shorthand for Southampton that effectively communicates a faddish yet feigned familiarity with the area. *Often pronounced with extra emphasis on the last syllable to express one's fabulous success and superiority (so-Hah!).* See **BriHa, EaHa.**

SoHi *abbr.* See **south of the highway.**

south of the highway *n.* **1.** The geographic area between the Montauk Highway and the Atlantic Ocean. —*adj.* **2.** Expensive; exclusive in reference to the value of real estate or the relative wealth of people with houses there. *"We have a cottage south of the highway."* Also **SoHi.** See **north of the highway.**

Southampton Slam *Recipe.* 1/2 oz. Green Creme de Menthe and 1/2 oz. Anisette with club soda.

Southampton Village *n.* A village with East Hampton envy, primarily because the median house price in East Hampton Village is double that of Southampton.

spandex rule

spandex rule *Adage.* "It is a privilege, not a right [to wear spandex]."

spec house *n.* A house designed and built for maximum profit without concern for function, quality, durability, ease of maintenance, etc. See **McMansion**.

spendthrift *n.* One who spends extravagantly on oneself, but is miserly when it comes to others. *e.g., A person who maintains a residence in the Hamptons, a townhouse in Manhattan and a collection of rare and exotic sports cars while dabbling in speculative Hamptons real estate ventures, yet who refuses to pay the $125 fee due for their child's extracurricular class.*

spirituality *n.* A higher form of arrogance. *A religious ceremony at Saint Andrew's Dune Church in Southampton, where ostentatious display of wealth in the form of jewelry, apparel and automobiles is de rigueur.*

spite fence *n.* A fence installed with the malicious intent of blocking one's view of or access to property.

spite hedge *n.* A hedge planted with the malicious intent of blocking one's view of or access to property.

spite house *n.* **1.** A house, addition, pool house, garage or other structure purposefully built to block the scenic view from a neighboring property. **2.** A trophy structure built solely to OUT-CASTLE another.

spleefcake *n.* A highly attractive but highly stoned man. Variation of **beefcake**.

spotlight effect *n.* **1.** The belief that others are paying closer attention to one's appearance and behavior than they really are or possibly could. **spotlighting** —*v.* **2.** Acting as if one is always the center of attention.

SPRICK *Acronym.* **spoiled rich kid** *n.* **1.** A child with a net worth larger than a U.S. Senator's and a MASTER OF THE UNIVERSE attitude. **2.** A MASTER OF THE UNIVERSE in training. See **bratitude**.

spud royalty See **Potato Royalty.**

staff *n.* A term used by seasonal visitors to describe local residents. Also **staph.**

staging *see* **house fluffing.**

Star Room, the *n.* A hyper-marketed Hamptons nightspot for TIN LIZZIES, A-LIST and TABLOID PEOPLE.

Starbucks See **Fourbucks**.

starchitect *n.* Architect to the stars. *e.g., Norman Jaffe.*

starfucked *adj.* **1.** Dazzled, or worse, by celebrities. *Paris Hilton in a micro mini skirt with no underwear, flashing patrons and staff at the Candy Kitchen in Bridgehampton.* **2.** Overcharged at Starbucks.

starstruck *adj.* Having received physical or economic damage from a celebrity. *e.g., The architect who was stiffed over $70,000 in fees for the design of a television sitcom star's Water Mill vacation house.* Also **starfucked**.

starter castle *n.* An overly large house built on a tiny piece of land.

starter jet *n.* A timeshare in a jet aircraft. *e.g., A $400,000 annual NetJets membership that includes 50 hours of flight time.*

starter marriage *n.* A short-lived first marriage that quickly ends in divorce.

starter Mercedes See **entry-lux**.

status *n.* A relative and constantly changing state or condition that is wholly dependent upon external circumstances. See **status quotient**.

status cymbal *n.* A blaringly loud or glaringly bright symbol of social position such as a six-figure Chopard diamond wrist watch, Lamborghini FUV, Lily Pond or Further Lane estate, etc. Also **bling**.

status panic *n.* The feeling of fear experienced upon finding oneself in an inferior social position. See **social insecurity.**

status points *n.* A system of scoring social position. *e.g., Driving an Aston Martin, 50 points; owning an Aston Martin, 500 points; wearing a tradesman's tool belt, 5,000 points.*

status quotient *n.* A complex, constantly variable equation performed on the fly to determine one's standing in any given social situation by comparing the cost, brand, vintage and condition of other's cars, clothing, jewelry, furnishings, housing, etc. with one's own.

Stop & Shop *Slang.* The Southampton Town Planning Department, where the financial interests of real estate developers are diligently catered to. See **candy store**.

stunting (stunt'·in) *Ebonics. v.* Displaying one's wealth. *e.g., Sean Combs' summer rental in the Hamptons.* See **White Party**.

sublebrity (sub'·leb·ri·tee) *n.* **1.** A lesser celebrity; a person on the B-list. *e.g., A writer or radio personality.* **2.** One who has received their 15 minutes of fame and is unlikely to get any more; a one-hit wonder. *e.g., Lizzie Grubman, Daniel Pelosi, the party-crashing club-hopping girls featured in the ABC television documentary "The Hamptons," etc.* **3.** A person who hangs around celebrities, hoping that some of it will rub off on them.

subsidy *n. Construction Industry.* A construction project with many change-orders. *"Move that window half an inch to the left."* See **renovation**.

suck down *n. v.* Attempt to curry favor from one's inferiors. *e.g., The Hamptons vacation house owner desperately in need of a* DRAIN SURGEON. Antonym **suck up**.

sunbird *n*. One who summers in the Hamptons and migrates to Florida for the winter.

surf and turf *n*. **1**. An oceanfront vacation property. **2**. Lobster *and* steak.

SUV *Acronym*. **Satan's Unholy Vehicle** *n*. **1**. The mandatory form of personal transportation in the Hamptons, championed by the PARVENU. **2**. A popular vehicle that's rate of gasoline consumption has forced American troops to secure and protect overseas oil supplies. **3**. Any four wheel drive car or truck that is never taken off-road. See **UAV**. **4**. *Oxymoron*. A vehicle that is used for neither sport nor utility.

swell *adj*. Full of oneself. *"He's a swell guy."* [OLD ENGLISH **sweall** (swollen)]

swinging dick *n*. **1**. A man who acts aggressively in all situations, especially those involving finance. **2**. A self-styled dickhead.

swiped out *adj*. **1**. Exhausted after a long day spent shopping. **2**. A credit card magstripe that has been worn out from extensive use.

tabloid people *pl. n.* Undesirable celebrities. See **shitterati**.

tag and release *v.* The act of picking up a potential love interest and setting them free prior to having sex, often practiced by husbands who don't want to cheat on their wives but who thrive on the ego boost the experience provides. Also **catch and release.**

talkitecture *n.* Discussion, in a public place such as a restaurant, of one's plans for a custom vacation house, loudly enough to insure that innocent bystanders will be subjected to a demonstration of one's fabulous wealth and success, often with the display of visual aids such as actual building plans. *A poor choice of status behaviors, especially if one's architect is not Santiago Calatrava, Norman Jaffe, Rem Koolhaas or Kenzo Tange.* See **designer babble**.

tanorexia *n.* A psychological disorder characterized by an abnormal fear of becoming pale, persistent tanning (natural or artificial) and an even toasty-brown complexion, advanced cases of which may be accompanied by malignant neoplasms of the skin.

tanscaping *n.* The art and practice of arranging or eliminating one's tan lines. See **fake and bake.**

tax holiday *n.* The practice of writing off the expense of purchasing or building an architect designed custom vacation house by claiming it as a business expense such as a satellite office, warehouse, corporate retreat, etc.

teardown *n.* The intent or inevitable result of most house purchases in the Hamptons.

tennis bracelet *n.* A circlet of diamonds or other precious stones worn on one's wrist while exercising or participating in a sporting event.

tennis pro *Euphemism.* Gigolo.

tennis racket *n.* **1.** High court fees. *"Ninety dollars for an hour of court time?!"* **2.** The noise, typically a grunt, that some players make every time they hit the ball. *"Unngh!"*

tennis pro

TGIT *Acronym.* **Thank God It's Tuesday.** A phrase used to indicate some small degree of relief that another long weekend is over and that traffic, congestion and the overall concentration of CIDIOTS will be at least marginally reduced until Thursday, when the next stampede of SHEEPLE headed to the Hamptons for an extended weekend begins.

thank queue *Expression.* Gratitude towards a person who has given one their place in a line.

Them *pl. n.* Seasonal visitors; tourists. *Origin: The 1954 science fiction film "Them' about giant mutant insects that devour everything in their path.* See **cidiot**. Also **They.** *e.g.,* "They're here."

there goes the neighborhood *Expression.* The change in property prices, social activity, etc., in a neighborhood when wealthy people move in.

thinking globally *v.* Contemplating the import of a classical marble bath from a 16th century Italian villa for the master bathroom in one's vacation house.

13 *n.* **1.** *Construction Industry.* A verbal code used to alert construction personnel that the general contractor has arrived at the site.

Formerly 22, until Benny Krupinski caught on. **2**. Bad luck. See **21**.

three-comma *Ebonics. adj.* Wealthy. *Derivation: the three commas in $1,000,000,000. Formerly* **two-comma**, *back when $1,000,000 was actually worth something.*

tick *n*. **1**. A persistent, blood-sucking parasite that travels from host to host, seeking a juicy bite. *e.g., A real estate broker.* **tick off** —*v*. **2**. Aggressively pursue new sources of sustenance. *e.g., Solicit new real estate sale listings.* **ticked off** —*adj*.

time *n*. The ultimate symbol of wealth, displayed simply with an abundance of patience. See **urgent haste**.

timed-out *Literal* "out of time." *adj*. **1**. Able to afford anything but the time necessary to acquire or enjoy it. —*n*. **2**. The extreme impatience demonstrated by anyone whose time is worth more than one's own.

tin lizzy *n*. **1**. False royalty. [OLD ENGLISH **tin**, (cheap, spurious) *and* **Lizzie** (nickname for Queen Elizabeth)] **2**. A Mercedes SUV like the one used by Lizzie Grubman to mow down late-night partiers. See **Lizzie Grubman Effect**.

3. A dose of low-quality drugs, often combined with alcohol. **4**. A speedball. —*v.* **5**. DWI. **6**. *Obsolete*. A cheap or dilapidated car.

tits *adj.* Terrific; really great. *"My new Porsche Cayenne is tits."*

tits up *adj.* Dead. *"Hello? Emergency towing? My new Porsche Cayenne is tits up on the LIE."* See **Farmer's Law.**

too much See **not enough**.

touch of class *n.* Meeting a celebrity, especially if there is physical contact. See **starstruck.**

tourist *n.* **1**. An amateur traveler. **2**. A person who, while traveling, ignores local culture and social customs. See **cidiot**. —*adj.* **3**. One who follows the crowd. See **sheeple**.

tourist bomb *n.* A full HAMPTON JITNEY.

tourist management *n.* A diet consisting primarily of humble pie. *The vital economic necessity of having to deal with masses of CIDIOTS and MASTERS OF THE UNIVERSE without offending them.* See **babysitter**.

tourist season *n*. A time of year that has locals reaching for their shotguns. *"If it's tourist season, why can't we shoot them?"*

tourist uniform *n*. Any style of dress that makes one instantly recognizable as a tourist. *A woman wearing a full black leather body suit to the Candy Kitchen at 8:30 Sunday morning.* See **Manhattan blonde**.

tourists syndrome *n*. A severe neurological disorder characterized by bizarre and apparently uncontrollable behavior which may include rapid movements and loud, irreverent vocalizations.

touron *n*. Half tourist, half moron.

tourrorist *n*. A vacationer whose behavior inspires fear and dread in others.

town *n*. **1**. Diminutive term for New York City. *"I'm going into town on Monday."* **2**. A small village or hamlet. *"I'm going into town on Monday."* See **downtown**.

trade parade *n*. Crushing daily commuter traffic consisting of people who work, but can't afford to live, in the Hamptons.

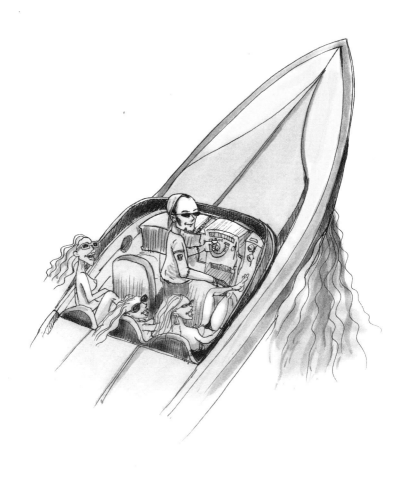

trustafarian

trashole (trash·hol') *n*. **1**. One who disposes of their weekend garbage in a restaurant or construction site dumpster or public refuse container prior to returning to their home in the city, a behavior justified by the $42 per month cost of garbage pickup that was not included in one's $50,000 summer rental, usually performed after dark on Sunday evenings or very early on Monday mornings in an attempt to avoid discovery. *The guy who puts his shit in your dumpster.* **2**. A person who dumps construction debris in the woods or at the beach to avoid carting fees. **trasholed** —*adj.*, **trasholing** —*v*. See **sanitrashion**.

trickle down theory *Economics.* The idea that if you feed a pig enough, something will pass through undigested for the rats to eat. Antonym **pour down theory**.

trump *v*. Solve a problem with brute application of money rather than intelligence.

trust slug *n*. One who has become pathetically self-centered, ignorant and indolent from living off the proceeds of a trust fund. See **acquired incompetence**.

trustafarian *n*. An unemployed person whose bohemian lifestyle is financed by a trust fund.

turn signals *n.* An optional feature that is invariably omitted from most luxury automobiles, presumably due to the cost. See **hamputee**.

tutor *n.* A babysitter with a high school diploma whose native language is English.

21 *n.* **1.** *Construction Industry.* A verbal code used to alert construction personnel that the project owner has arrived at the site. **2.** Blackjack. See **13**.

UAV *Acronym.* **Urban Assault Vehicle** *n.* A large, heavy SUV that is never, ever, driven off-road. See **land yacht**.

***über* rich** *adj.* **1**. More than OBSCENELY RICH. **2**. Financial wealth beyond conception or calculation. **3**. Wealth beyond description in the English language.

uh-oh seven See **James Blonde**.

un-Hampton, the *n. Obsolete.* Sag Harbor.

universal law of construction *Adage.* "Fast, cheap, or nice; pick any two." A concept that is simply impossible for any MASTER OF THE UNIVERSE to grasp. *"Fast and cheap? It isn't going to be very nice."*

unobtainium *n.* **1**. An item so expensive or otherwise difficult to obtain that ownership is precluded by all but a few. —*adj*. **2**. An exceedingly rare or one of a kind object. *An original, unaltered, Norman Jaffe designed house in the Hamptons.* **3**. Impossibly difficult to acquire. Antonym OBTAINIUM.

unreal estate *n*. Property in the Hamptons.

unvitation *n*. **1**. An empty invitation, one that is not meant to be accepted. *e.g., An invitation delivered at the last minute or after determining that one is unavailable at that particular time.* **2**. An invitation pointedly given to someone in your presence and not to you.

up-island *adj*. **1**. Low-class; uneducated; unsophisticated. **2**. Poor quality; unfashionable. *"They are so up-island."* See **west of the canal.**

upgrade *v*. **1**. To parlay rapidly escalating real estate prices into ever bigger houses in the Hamptons. **2**. To dump a current spouse or lover for one perceived to be richer or more attractive, preferably both.

upscale *adj*. **1**. Pretentious. **2**. Appealing to the uneducated palates of the nouveau riche. —*n*. **3**. A marketing term intended to increase the price of a product or service by offering an intangible benefit such as name branding or association to luxury, which imparts a sense of comfort to socially insecure shoppers. *"This upscale property, listed at $4.95 million, has five bedrooms, six baths, a 40 foot swimming pool and a driveway view of the Atlantic Golf Club from its prestigious 1.2 acre site off Noyac Path."*

upside down house *n*. **1**. A house with bedrooms located on the main floor and common living areas located on the second floor, often so as to maximize the use and value of a VIEW SHAFT. **2**. Any badly designed house.

urgent haste *n*. The projection of an air of importance. *e.g., The man who offered increasing amounts of money in exchange for a place in the line in front of him at the Village Cheese Shop in Southampton until a man in front of him said, "Sir, there are people in this line with more money and less time than you."* See **status quotient**. **2**. A frantic behavioral display exemplified by those whose vacation is coming to an end and are busily cramming every possible recreational activity, social event and celebrity attended gala into the final few days before their summer rental expires. See **timed-out**.

vacation home *Oxymoron. n.* **1.** A house that nobody lives in. *A home is where one lives, while a vacation house is a place that one visits, typically on holidays.* **2.** A symbol of and temple to one's wealth. Also **cashtle**. **3.** Part of a diversified investment portfolio.

vacation house *n.* A massive, sprawling hotel-like structure designed for weekend and holiday get-aways that includes accommodations and parking for a host of guests and recreational facilities such as a tennis court, swimming pool, beach access, etc.

value based pricing *n. Obsolete.* The practice of charging customers based on one's set of personal values. *e.g., The Water Mill auto mechanic who overcharged his wealthy customers so that he could undercharge his poor ones.* See **local price**.

Vulcan eyebrows

vanity pricing *n.* Setting the price of a product or service at a level reassuring to UPSCALE consumers. *If it's cheap it can't be good.* See **wallet screw**.

vanity sizing *n.* The tendency of real estate brokers to describe the size of a house by including the square footage of the basement, garage, attic, decks and patios, etc.

view shaft *n.* **1.** The narrow sliver of view between surrounding structures or landscaping through which a pond, bay, ocean or other natural feature can be glimpsed. **2.** A feature that adds considerable value to Hamptons real estate. **view shafted** —*adj.* **3.** Having lost one's view of the ocean or other natural feature by the construction of a SPEC HOUSE, McMANSION, SPITE HEDGE, etc., with a corresponding decrease in the resale value of one's property.

virtual reality *n.* The insulated condition or fantasy state in which the wealthy live.

voice lift *n.* Cosmetic surgery of the vocal cord designed to make a person's voice sound younger.

Vulcan eyebrows *n.* Evidence of recent non-surgical dermatology. See **frozen asset**.

Vulgaria *n.* Any place where conspicuous display of wealth is de rigueur. *e.g., The Hamptons, Aspen, Boca Raton, Beverly Hills, St. Barts, St. Tropez, etc.*

Vulgarian *n.* **1.** A crude, rude and offensive person, especially one who makes a conspicuous display of wealth. Also **boor**. **2.** A native or inhabitant of Vulgaria. —*adj.* **3.** Of or relating to Vulgaria or its people, language, or culture.

W

waitron *n.* A lazy, slow, clumsy or otherwise inept waiter or waitress. *A dumb waiter.* Conflation of **waiter** and **moron**.

walkout *n. Food service.* A person who leaves a restaurant without paying. Antonym **walk-in**.

wallet screw *v.* Charge as much as possible, ostensibly to reassure a customer of the value of their purchase. See **snob effect**.

waterfront *adj.* A marketing term used to describe property that is not on the ocean, often applied to land adjacent to a recharge basin or an area that routinely floods.

Water Mill *n.* A speed bump between Southampton Village and Bridgehampton.

watershed *Landscaping. n.* The art of producing lush green lawns through over-watering and over-fertilizing solely in order to justify a minimum of two lawn cuttings per week through November. See **irrigation system**.

waterview *adj.* A marketing term used to describe property from which a water feature other than the ocean is visible, often through a narrow VIEW SHAFT, raising the property value considerably. See **view shaft**.

wealthy *adj.* 1. Not merely rich, but loaded. **2.** Insolent and arrogant.

weekend warrior *n.* A person who bravely battles choking traffic, overbooked restaurants, massive crowds, absurdly high prices, etc. on a weekend holiday in the Hamptons.

well-off *adj.* When others are happy to see you go.

west of the canal *n.* **1.** That portion of Long Island defined geographically as being west of the Shinnecock Canal. —*adj.* **2.** Cheap; shoddy. **3.** Geographically undesirable. Antonym **east of the canal**. See **up-island**.

Westhampton *Literal* "West of the Hamptons." *n.* **1.** A faux Hampton. See **west of the canal**. **2.** The last refuge of Disco.

whale pod *n.* A group of young women purposefully displaying their WHALE TAILS above

whale pod with chum slick

the waist line of low-riding pants. *Whale pods are often trailed by a* CHUM SLICK.

whale tail *n.* **1.** The waistband and rear strap of a woman's thong underwear, visible above the waistline of her pants, shorts, or skirt, so called because of its resemblance to a whale's tail rising from the ocean. **2.** An oversized rear spoiler found on cars such as the Porsche 911SC.

wheel estate *n.* **1.** An SUV so large that its size is defined in acreage. **2.** An investment-caliber collection of automobiles.

White Party *n.* **1.** An annual Hamptons party with an all-white dress code that is hosted by Sean Combs and other rap and hip-hop celebrities. **2.** A political movement that advocates sending all non-white people back to their ancestor's countries of origin. **3.** The Republican Party.

white plague See **consumption.**

white trash *adj.* **1.** Wealthy people who exhibit boorish or anti-social behavior. *Derivation: Lizzie Grubman, who screamed "white trash" shortly before reversing over 16 people at Conscience Point Inn in her father's black Mercedes SUV.* See **Lizzie Grubman Effect.** —*n.* **2.** Expensive goods in perfect condition that are thrown away simply because they are dirty or out of style. *The detritus of the rich.*

wifestyle *n*. **1**. The standard of living set by one's wife. **wifestyled** —*adj*. **2**. Forced to live, often uncomfortably, under a bizarre set of rules intended to preserve the exact appearance of one's apartment, vacation house, or wife. **wifestyler** —*n*. **3**. A woman obsessed with the redecoration of her apartment, vacation house or self.

winner *n*. One who has successfully managed to cheat another out of money or property. *e.g., The man at a cocktail party who proudly boasted about screwing the builder of his Bridgehampton vacation house out of $150,000.*

yard sailor

yama *Japanese, literal* "mountain." *adj.* Excellent; superior. *Derivation: Yama-Q Restaurant in* BRIDGEHAMPTON.

yachtzi *n.* A smugly superior, domineering and aggressive boat owner, who can only be shut up (and then only temporarily) by the appearance of an even larger and more expensive boat, at which point the yachtzi will turn green with envy. See **status quotient**. Conflation of **yacht** and **nazi**.

yard sailor *n.* **1**. One who frequents yard sales. **2**. A bargain hunter. See **mize**. **yard sailing** —*v.*

yard sale *n.* **1**. The scene of an accident in which the victim's belongings are scattered over a wide area. **2**. A cash-basis home-operated pseudo-antique business, usually supplied from other yard sales or the landfill. See **Caldor East**. **3**. A magnet that attracts CIDIOTS and MIZERS.

4. A technique used to trick others into paying for the opportunity to haul away one's trash. See **recycle**.

yardie *n*. **1.** A landscape laborer, often an illegal immigrant. See **four footer**. **2.** A gang member, drug dealer or violent criminal.

you said ... *Expression*. A prelude to a lie used as a form of negotiation, usually an attempt to bully one into accepting less money for a product or service by lying about the initially agreed cost, delivery schedule, etc. *"You said it was only going to cost $500" or "You said it would be delivered Thursday."* Also **but you said** ...

yuppie porn *n*. Magazines catering to obsessively consumptive UPSCALE lifestyles. *e.g.,* *Condé Nast Traveler, Architectural Digest, Vogue, Dupont Registry of Fine Homes, etc.*

FURTHER READING

Class: A Guide Through the American Status System, by Paul Fussell, Summit Books, 1983. The only true detailed examination of the American class system. This is one of many texts that should be required reading in high school, as it not only points out the similarities between the top and bottom-out-of-sights but also the absurdity of the entire class structure and the fallacies upon which it is built. According to *The New York Times*, "shrewd" and "frighteningly acute".

Richistan: A Journey Through the American Wealth Boom and the Lives of the New Rich, by Robert Frank, Crown, 2007. An evenhanded journalistic travelogue into the world the other 0.05% lives in. A good read that shows just how far from the rest of us the wealthy really are.

The Natural History of the Rich: A Field Guide, by Richard Conniff, W. W. Norton & Company, 2002. An insightful and absolutely hilarious behavioral comparison of the sub-species of *homo sapiens* known as the wealthy *(homo sapiens peconiosus)* with various animal species including birds and primates.

Theory of the Leisure Class, by Thorstein Veblen, 1899. Establishing the original concept of conspicuous consumption, Veblen's classic guide to the behavior of the wealthy is the penultimate reference for all who have followed. Still fresh and accurate a century later.

The Nanny Diaries: A Novel, by Emma McLaughlin and Nicola Kraus, St. Martin's, 2003. The reason that nannies now have contracts with non-disclosure clauses. A gaggingly delicious inside view of the lifestyle and behavior of an entirely overloaded New York City couple.

The Devil's Dictionary, by Ambrose Bierce, 1911 (republished Bloomsbury, 2003). Critical social commentary in the form of a collection of cynical definitions that Bierce published from 1881 to 1886 in the *Wasp*, a weekly journal in San Francisco, and the model on which *The Hamptons Dictionary* is based. While Bierce didn't create neologisms, he redefined existing words to have a far more critical and often accurate meaning. *The Devil's Dictionary* shows that the concept and practice of spin, though uncoined, was alive and well a full century ago.

Wealth Addiction, by Philip Slater, E. P. Dutton, 1980. By defining the all-consuming quest for riches as a disease, Slater puts a timely twist on values in the age of globalization. He also broaches the idea that accumulation of wealth is an evolutionary adaptation to a domesticated society in which hunting, agriculture and other direct living skills have been rendered obsolete.

The Naked Ape, by Desmond Morris, McGraw-Hill, 1967. No matter how high we aspire, the truth is that we are simply primates that have gone down a slightly different evolutionary branch. Morris, a zoologist and former curator of the London Zoo, points out how closely related we remain to our genetic ancestors, who often seem downright civilized in comparison to their more highly evolved cousins.

The Bonfire of the Vanities, by Tom Wolfe, Farrar, Straus and Giroux, 1987. Self-interest reigns supreme in this fictional tale of a self-appointed master of the universe's fall from grace. Also the basis for an utterly vapid movie of the same name with Tom Hanks and Bruce Willis.

The End Of The Hamptons: Scenes From The Class Struggle In America's Paradise, by Corey Dolgon, New York University Press, 2005. A sociologist's dry overview of the Hamptons melting pot from robber barons to the illegal immigrants who grease the wheels of progress.

BACKWORD

As always, my wife Mary deserves credit for enduring, not just me in general, but those peculiar quests upon which I often find myself. In the case of this one, she never came around to liking the project but continued to feed and house me anyway.

My daughter Aiyana has, as ever, been most supportive and encouraging, catching the creative spirit and offering numerous words, suggestions and even cover designs. I truly hope that she finds me to be as helpful and encouraging with all of her projects. Even more than that, I hope that being raised in such a twisted social environment doesn't have too many detrimental effects upon her.

Sincere thanks are owed to the many people who contributed to this project including John *"do you take cash?"* Battle, Chris *"never count someone else's money"* Brancato, Rob *"paper the file"* Camerino, Bill *"disturbia"* Chaleff, Wendy *"tag and release"* Chamberlin, Len *"BANANA"* Davenport, Katherine *"tennis racket"* DeGroot, James *"Hamptons Shuffle"* DeMartis, Paul *"Slick and Phony"* D'Andrea, Jameson *"power bitch"* Ellis, Ian *"Manhattan blond"* Evans, Jan *"hedge fund"* Flack, Marilee *"mommiac"* Foster, Shira *"free rider"* Kalish, Jennifer *"starchitect"* Keil, Anthony *"cloakie"* Leichter, Joseph *"creeping Hamptonism"* Marcincuk, Marcia *"hamputee"* Mitrowski, John *"MVA"* Muse, Raun *"Salvation Armani"* Norquist, Janet *"spleefcake"* Sadowski, Sara-Jo *"Vulgarian"* Strickland, Anthony *"pillow talk"* Szalkowski, Nathaniel *"fresh out"* Thayer, Nancy *"spandex rule"* Thompson, the *centsless* guy at Iron Horse Graphics and the town cop who described *Hamptonite* without the slightest trace of humor. If I have forgotten to acknowledge a contributor here, it is not with malice, but error, and please accept my sincere thanks.

Thanks are also due (in a clearly ironic and somewhat perverted way) to the sad guy who went ballistically *mobile* while pushing his young child in a stroller down Job's Lane; the poor fellow who gave a *command performance*, setting off the alarm in the Range Rover he had just locked himself out of (directly in front of a crowd seated on the sidewalk at Café Reggio); and all too many other *cidiots* and *locals* alike who have gone out of their way to demonstrate the behaviors documented here.

Acknowledgement is most certainly owed to Ted Pettus, not only for his encouragement but also for his prescient suggestion that I self-publish. After only a few years of trying to do it the other way I finally followed his advice, and as he predicted, a publisher came calling. Thanks and condolences to Gary Baddeley at The Disinformation Company for seeing what no other publisher did and falling into that carefully laid trap.

A grateful thank you goes to proofreader Kendra *"high roller"* Eager. My deepest appreciation goes to Gabrielle *"trashole"* Brooks for outstanding enthusiastic support, assistance and professional guidance in my self-publishing venture. A truly special thanks is owed to Carla *"frozen asset"* Riccio, who provided much encouragement, editing and a number of really juicy terms. Thanks also and a sincere "well done" to Plinio Marcos Pinto, whose spectacular illustrations bring to life a number of terms presented here.

Finally, none of this would have been possible without the experience of growing up in the office of my father, *starchitect* Norman *"shake and bake"* Jaffe, whose often painfully acquired insight into the behavior of the wealthy underlies much of what is documented here.

Miles Jaffe

Author **Miles Jaffe** is an artist, satirist, industrial designer and RISD graduate working out of a studio and prototype shop in Bridgehampton, New York. He has earned both accolades and notoriety for his 2001 satirical website *Nuke The Hamptons*, which received widespread international media attention.

Jaffe's firm *Complete Fabrications* specializes in the design and execution of a wide range of creative projects from architecture, furniture and product design to graphic design and new media, some of which can be seen at online at www.milesjaffe.com.

Plinio Marcos Pinto is an illustrator and graphic artist working in a studio in Orlando, Florida. Born and raised in Brazil, he studied at the Ringling College of Art and Design in Sarasota, where he won a Certificate of Merit from the Society of Illustrators with work published and displayed at SOI gallery in New York.

Plinio's clients include Playboy Enterprises, Inc., *Dallas Observer*, *Orlando Weekly* and the *Loyola College Magazine* in Maryland. He also co-owns and is art director for the American Brazilian community's *Zest Magazine*.

INDEX

SUBMIT A WORD

Have a word or
expression to contribute,
or a behavior that needs one?

Send it to
word@hamptonsdictionary.com

BUY THE BOOK

Laughter is the perfect gift.

www.hamptonsdictionary.com